Bushido

The Soul of Japan

Bushido

>>>>>>>>>>>>>>>>>>>><<<<<<<<<<<<<<<<<<<<

The Soul of Japan

Inazo Nitobe

TUTTLE PUBLISHING
BOSTON   RUTLAND, VT   TOKYO

Distributed by

North America, Latin America, and Europe
Tuttle Publishing
Distribution Center
Airport Industrial Park
364 Innovation Drive
North Clarendon, VT 05759-9436
Tel: (802) 773-8930
Fax: (802) 773-6993
Email: info@tuttlepublishing.com

Asia Pacific
Berkeley Books Pte. Ltd.
130 Joo Seng Road
#06-01/03 Olivine Building
Singapore 368357
Tel: (65) 6280-3320
Fax: (65) 6280-6290
Email: inquiries@periplus.com.sg

Japan
Tuttle Publishing
Yaekari Bldg., 3F
5-4-12 Ōsaki, Shinagawa-ku
Tokyo 141-0032
Tel: (03) 5437-0171
Fax: (03) 35437-0755
Email: tuttle-sales@gol.com

08 07 06 05 04 03   9 8 7 6 5 4

Printed in the United States of America

TO MY BELOVED UNCLE

TOKITOSHI OTA

WHO TAUGHT ME TO REVERE THE PAST

AND

TO ADMIRE THE DEEDS OF THE SAMURAI

I DEDICATE

THIS LITTLE BOOK

CONTENTS

Contents

PUBLISHER'S FOREWORD

THIS attractive little book explaining the "soul of Japan" has had a remarkable welcome and response since it was first published in 1905. Today the demand is as great as ever despite the "Westernization" of Japan.

Possibly the chief reason for the demand is that the book answered and continues to answer, for the Japanese as well as the Westerner, the reason why certain ideas and customs prevail in Japan.

Bushido has been variously defined, but it would seem that the definition most generally accepted is that Bushido is the unwritten code of laws governing the lives and conduct of the nobles of Japan, equivalent in many ways to the European chivalry.

The knights and nobles of feudal Japan were

the samurai, retainers of the daimyo. Thus, Bushido was the code of conduct of the samurai, the aristocratic warrior class which arose during the wars of the 12th century between the Taira and Minamoto clans—and came to glorious fruition in the Tokugawa period.

The samurai cultivated the martial virtues, were indifferent to death and pain in their loyalty to their overlords. Samurai were privileged to wear two swords, which were in turn "the soul of the samurai," according to Nitobe.

Bushido presents the cause of Japan in simple but sincere and very readable terms. The author illustrates the points he presents with parallel examples from European history and literature. Finally and foremost, he believes in the law written in the heart. This book was originally published in 1905 by G. P. Putnam's Sons, New York.

PREFACE TO THE FIRST EDITION

ABOUT ten years ago, while spending a few days under the hospitable roof of the distinguished Belgian jurist, the lamented M. de Laveleye, our conversation turned during one of our rambles, to the subject of religion. "Do you mean to say," asked the venerable professor, "that you have no religious instruction in your schools?" On my replying in the negative, he suddenly halted in astonishment, and in a voice which I shall not easily forget, he repeated "No religion! How do you impart moral education?" The question stunned me at the time. I could give no ready answer, for the moral precepts I learned in my childhood days were not given in schools; and not until I began to analyse the different elements that formed my notions of right and wrong, did I find that it was Bushido that breathed them into my nostrils.

The direct inception of this little book is due to the frequent queries put by my wife as to the reasons why such and such ideas and customs prevail in Japan.

In my attempts to give satisfactory replies to M. de Laveleye and to my wife, I found that without understanding feudalism and Bushido,[1] the moral ideas of present Japan are a sealed volume.

Taking advantage of enforced idleness on account of long illness, I put down in the order now presented to the public some of the answers given in our household conversation. They consist mainly of what I was taught and told in my youthful days, when feudalism was still in force.

Between Lafcadio Hearn and Mrs. Hugh Fraser on one side and Sir Ernest Satow and

---

[1] Pronounced Boóshee-doh'. In putting Japanese words and names into English, Hepburn's rule is followed, that the vowels should be used as in European languages, and the consonants as in English.

Professor Chamberlain on the other, it is indeed discouraging to write anything Japanese in English. The only advantage I have over them is that I can assume the attitude of a personal defendant, while these distinguished writers are at best solicitors and attorneys. I have often thought,—"Had I their gift of language, I would present the cause of Japan in more eloquent terms!" But one who speaks in a borrowed tongue should be thankful if he can just make himself intelligible.

All through the discourse I have tried to illustrate whatever points I have made with parallel examples from European history and literature, believing that these will aid in bringing the subject nearer to the comprehension of foreign readers.

Should any of my allusions to religious subjects and to religious workers be thought slighting, I trust my attitude toward Christianity itself will not be questioned. It is with ecclesiastical methods and with the forms which obscure the teachings of Christ, and not with the teachings themselves, that

I have little sympathy. I believe in the religion taught by Him and handed down to us in the New Testament, as well as in the law written in the heart. Further, I believe that God hath made a testament which may be called "old" with every people and nation,—Gentile or Jew, Christian or Heathen. As to the rest of my theology, I need not impose upon the patience of the public.

In concluding this preface, I wish to express my thanks to my friend Anna C. Hartshorne for many valuable suggestions.

I. N.

INTRODUCTION

AT the request of his publishers, to whom Dr. Nitobe has left some freedom of action concerning prefatory matter, I am glad to offer a few sentences of introduction to this new edition of *Bushido*, for readers of English everywhere. I have been acquainted with the author for over fifteen years, indeed, but, in a measure at least, with his subject during forty-five years.

It was in 1860, in Philadelphia (where, in 1847, I saw the *Susquehanna*, Commodore Perry's flagship launched), that I looked on my first Japanese and met members of the Embassy from Yedo. I was mightily impressed with these strangers, to whom Bushido was a living code of ideals and manners. Later, during three years at Rutgers College, New Brunswick, N. J., I was among scores of young men from Nippon, whom I taught or

knew as fellow-students. I found that Bushido, about which we often talked, was a
superbly winsome thing. As illustrated in
the lives of these future governors, diplomat-
ists, admirals, educators, and bankers, yes,
even in the dying hours of more than one who
"fell on sleep" in Willow Grove Cemetery,
the perfume of this most fragrant flower of
far-off Japan was very sweet. Never shall I
forget how the dying samurai lad, Kusakabe,
when invited to the noblest of services and
the greatest of hopes, made answer: "Even
if I could know your Master, Jesus, I should
not offer Him only the dregs of a life." So,
"on the banks of the old Raritan," in athletic
sports, in merry jokes at the supper table when
contrasting things Japanese and Yankee,
and in the discussion of ethics and ideals,
I felt quite willing to take the "covert missionary retort," about which my friend
Charles Dudley Warner once wrote. At
some points, codes of ethics and proprieties
differed, but rather in dots or tangents than
as occultation or eclipse. As their own poet

wrote—was it a thousand years ago?—when in crossing a moor the dew-laden flowers brushed by his robe left their glittering drops on his brocade, "On account of its perfume, I brush not this moisture from my sleeve." Indeed, I was glad to get out of ruts, which are said to differ from graves only by their length. For, is not comparison the life of science and culture? Is it not true that, in the study of languages, ethics, religions, and codes of manners, "he who knows but one knows none"?

Called, in 1870, to Japan as pioneer educator to introduce the methods and spirit of the American public-school system, how glad I was to leave the capital, and at Fukui, in the province of Echizen, see pure feudalism in operation! There I looked on Bushido, not as an exotic, but in its native soil. In daily life I realised that Bushido, with its *cha-no-yu*, *jū-jŭtsŭ* ("jiu-jitsu"), *hara-kiri*, polite prostrations on the mats and genuflections on the street, rules of the sword and road, all leisurely salutations and politest moulds of speech, canons of art and conduct, as well as heroisms for wife, maid, and child, formed the universal creed and praxis of all the gentry in the castled city and province. In it, as a living school of thought and life, girl and boy alike were trained. What Dr. Nitobe received as an inheritance, had breathed into his nostrils, and writes about so gracefully and forcibly, with such grasp, insight, and breadth of view, I saw. Japanese feudalism "died without the sight" of its ablest exponent and most convincing defender. To him it is as wafted fragrance. To me it was "the plant and flower of light."

Hence, living under and being in at the death of feudalism, the body of Bushido, I can bear witness to the essential truth of Dr. Nitobe's descriptions, so far as they go, and to the faithfulness of his analysis and generalisations. He has limned with masterly art and reproduced the colouring of the picture which a thousand years of Japanese literature reflects so gloriously. The Knightly Code grew up during a millenium of evolution, and our author lovingly notes the blooms that have starred the path trodden by millions of noble souls, his countrymen.

Critical study has but deepened my own sense of the potency and value of Bushido to the nation. He who would understand twentieth-century Japan must know something of its roots in the soil of the past. Even if now as invisible to the present generation in Nippon as to the alien, the philosophic student reads the results of to-day in the stored energies of ages gone. The sunbeams of unrecorded time have laid the strata out of which Japan now digs her foot-pounds of impact for war or peace. All the spiritual senses are keen in those nursed by Bushido. The crystalline lump has dissolved in the sweetened cup, but the delicacy of the flavour remains to cheer. In a word, Bushido has obeyed the higher law enunciated by One whom its own exponent salutes and confesses his Master—"Except a grain of corn die, it abideth alone; but if it die it bringeth forth much fruit."

Has Dr. Nitobe idealised Bushido? Rather, we ask, how could he help doing so? He calls himself "defendant." In all creeds, cults, and systems, while the ideal grows, exemplars and exponents vary. Gradual cumulation and slow attainment of harmony is the law. Bushido never reached a final goal. It was too much alive, and it died at last only in its splendour and strength. The clash of the world's movement—for so we name the rush of influences and events which followed Perry and Harris—with feudalism in Japan, did not find Bushido an embalmed mummy, but a living soul. What it really met was the quickening spirit of humanity. Then the less was blessed of the greater. Without losing the best in her own history and civilisation, Japan, following her own noble precedents, first adopted and then adapted the choicest the world had to offer. Thus her opportunity to bless Asia and the race became unique, and grandly she has embraced it—"in diffusion ever more intense." To-day, not only are our gardens, our art, our homes enriched by the flowers, the pictures, and the pretty things of Japan, whether "trifles of a moment or triumphs for all time," but in physical culture, in public hygiene, in lessons for peace and war, Japan has come to us with her hands gift-laden.

Not only in his discourse as advocate and counsel for the defence, but as prophet and wise householder, rich in things new and old, our author is able to teach us. No man in Japan has united the precepts and practice of his own Bushido more harmoniously in life and toil, labour and work, craft of hand and of pen, culture of the soil and of the soul. Illuminator of Dai Nippon's past, Dr. Nitobe is a true maker of the New Japan. In Formosa, the empire's new accretion, as in Kioto, he is the scholar and practical man, at home in newest science and most ancient diligence.

This little book on Bushido is more than a weighty message to the Anglo-Saxon nations. It is a notable contribution to the solution of this century's grandest problem—the reconciliation and unity of the East and the West.

There were of old many civilisations: in the better world coming there will be one. Already the terms "Orient" and "Occident," with all their freight of mutual ignorance and insolence, are ready to pass away. As the efficient middle term between the wisdom and communism of Asia and the energy and individualism of Europe and America, Japan is already working with resistless power.

Instructed in things ancient and modern and cultured in the literatures of the world, Dr. Nitobe herein shows himself admirably fitted for a congenial task. He is a true interpreter and reconciler. He need not and does not apologise for his own attitude toward the Master whom he has long loyally followed. What scholar, familiar with the ways of the Spirit and with the history of the race as led by man's Infinite Friend, but must in all religions put difference between the teachings of the Founder and the original documents and the ethnic, rationalistic, and ecclesiastical additions and accretions? The doctrine of the testaments, hinted at in the author's preface, is the teaching of Him who came not to destroy, but to fulfil. Even in Japan, Christianity, unwrapped from its foreign mould and matting, will cease being an exotic and strike its roots deep in the soil on which Bushido has grown. Stripped alike of its swaddling bands and its foreign regimentals, the church of the Founder will be as native as the air.

WILLIAM ELLIOT GRIFFIS.

ITHACA, May, 1905.

" That way
Over the mountain, which who stands upon
Is apt to doubt if it be indeed a road;
While if he views it from the waste itself,
Up goes the line there, plain from base to brow,
Not vague, mistakable! What's a break or two
Seen from the unbroken deserts either side?
And then (to bring in fresh philosophy)
What if the breaks themselves should prove at last
The most consummate of contrivances
To train a man's eye, teach him what is faith?"

ROBERT BROWNING,
Bishop Blougram's Apology.

"There are, if I may so say, three powerful spirits,
which have, from time to time, moved on the face of
the waters, and given a predominant impulse to the
moral sentiments and energies of mankind.   These
are the spirits of liberty, of religion, and of honor.

HALLAM,
Europe in the Middle Ages.

"Chivalry is itself the poetry of life."

SCHLEGEL,
Philosophy of History.

BUSHIDO

CHAPTER I

BUSHIDO AS AN ETHICAL SYSTEM

CHIVALRY is a flower no less indigenous to the soil of Japan than its emblem, the cherry blossom; nor is it a dried-up specimen of an antique virtue preserved in the herbarium of our history. It is still a living object of power and beauty among us; and if it assumes no tangible shape or form, it not the less scents the moral atmosphere, and makes us aware that we are still under its potent spell. The conditions of society which brought it forth and nourished it have long disappeared; but as those far-off stars which once were and are not, still continue to shed their rays upon us, so the light of chivalry, which was a child of feudalism, still illuminates our moral path, surviving its mother institution. It is a pleasure to me to reflect upon this subject in the language of Burke, who uttered the well-known touching eulogy over the neglected bier of its European prototype.

It argues a sad defect of information concerning the Far East, when so erudite a scholar as Dr. George Miller did not hesitate to affirm that chivalry, or any other similar institution, has never existed either among the nations of antiquity or among the modern Orientals.[1] Such ignorance, however, is amply excusable, as the third edition of the good Doctor's work appeared the same year that Commodore Perry was knocking at the portals of our exclusivism. More than a decade later, about the time that our feudalism was in the last throes of existence, Carl Marx, writing his *Capital*, called the attention of his readers to the peculiar advantage of studying the social and political

[1] *History Philosophically Illustrated* (3d ed., 1853), vol. ii., p. 2.

institutions of feudalism, as then to be seen
in living form only in Japan. I would
likewise point the Western historical and
ethical student to the study of chivalry in
the Japan of the present.

Enticing as is an historical disquisition on
the comparison between European and Japanese feudalism and chivalry, it is not the
purpose of this paper to enter into it at
length. My attempt is rather to relate
firstly, the origin and sources of our chivalry;
secondly, its character and teaching; *thirdly*,
its influence among the masses; and, *fourthly*,
the continuity and permanence of its influence.
Of these several points, the first will be only
brief and cursory, or else I should have to
take my readers into the devious paths of our
national history; the second will be dwelt
upon at greater length, as being most likely
to interest students of International Ethics
and Comparative Ethology in our ways of
thought and action; and the rest will be
dealt with as corollaries.

The Japanese word which I have roughly

rendered Chivalry, is, in the original, more expressive than Horsemanship. *Bu-shi-do* means literally Military - Knight - Ways— the ways which fighting nobles should observe in their daily life as well as in their vocation; in a word, the "Precepts of Knighthood," the *noblesse oblige* of the warrior class. Having thus given its literal significance, I may be allowed henceforth to use the word in the original. The use of the original term is also advisable for this reason, that a teaching so circumscribed and unique, engendering a cast of mind and character so peculiar, so local, must wear the badge of its singularity on its face; then, some words have a national *timbre* so expressive of race characteristics that the best of translators can do them but scant justice, not to say positive injustice and grievance. Who can improve by translation what the German "*Gemüth*" signifies, or who does not feel the difference between the two words verbally so closely allied as the English *gentleman* and the French *gentilhomme?*

Bushido, then, is the code of moral principles which the knights were required or instructed to observe. It is not a written code; at best it consists of a few maxims handed down from mouth to mouth or coming from the pen of some well-known warrior or savant. More frequently it is a code unuttered and unwritten, possessing all the more the powerful sanction of veritable deed, and of a law written on the fleshly tablets of the heart. It was founded not on the creation of one brain, however able, or on the life of a single personage, however renowned. It was an organic growth of decades and centuries of military career. It, perhaps, fills the same position in the history of ethics that the English Constitution does in political history; yet it has had nothing to compare with the Magna Charta or the Habeas Corpus Act. True, early in the seventeenth century Military Statutes (*Buké Hatto*) were promulgated; but their thirteen short articles were taken up mostly with marriages, castles, leagues, etc., and didactic regulations were but meagerly touched upon.

We cannot, therefore, point out any definite time and place and say, "Here is its fountain-head." Only as it attains consciousness in the feudal age, its origin, in respect to time, may be identified with feudalism. But feudalism itself is woven of many threads, and Bushido shares its intricate nature. As in England the political institutions of feudalism may be said to date from the Norman Conquest, so we may say that in Japan its rise was simultaneous with the ascendancy of Yoritomo, late in the twelfth century. As, however, in England, we find the social elements of feudalism far back in the period previous to William the Conqueror, so, too, the germs of feudalism in Japan had been long existent before the period I have mentioned.

Again, in Japan as in Europe, when feudalism was formally inaugurated, the professional class of warriors naturally came into prominence. These were known as *samurai*, meaning literally, like the old English *cniht* (knecht, knight), guards or attendants—

resembling in character the *soldurii*, whom
Cæsar mentioned as existing in Aquitania,
or the *comitati*, who, according to Tacitus,
followed Germanic chiefs in his time; or, to
take a still later parallel, the *milites medii*
that one reads about in the history of Mediæval Europe. A Sinico-Japanese word
Bu-ké or *Bu-shi* (Fighting Knights) was also
adopted in common use. They were a
privileged class, and must originally have been
a rough breed who made fighting their vocation. This class was naturally recruited, in
a long period of constant warfare, from the
manliest and the most adventurous, and all
the while the process of elimination went on,
the timid and the feeble being sorted out, and
only "a rude race, all masculine, with brutish
strength," to borrow Emerson's phrase,
surviving to form families and the ranks of
the samurai. Coming to profess great honour
and great privileges, and correspondingly
great responsibilities, they soon felt the need
of a common standard of behaviour, especially
as they were always on a belligerent footing

and belonged to different clans. Just as physicians limit competition among themselves by professional courtesy, just as lawyers sit in courts of honour in cases of violated etiquette; so must also warriors possess some resort for final judgment on their misdemeanours.

Fair play in fight! What fertile germs of morality lie in this primitive sense of savagery and childhood. Is it not the root of all military and civic virtue? We smile (as if we had outgrown it!) at the boyish desire of the small Britisher, Tom Brown, "to leave behind him the name of a fellow who never bullied a little boy or turned his back on a big one." And yet, who does not know that this desire is the corner-stone on which moral structures of mighty dimensions can be reared? May I not go even so far as to say that the gentlest and most peace-loving of religions endorses this aspiration? The desire of Tom is the basis on which the greatness of England is largely built, and it will not take us long to discover that *Bushido*

does not stand on a lesser pedestal. If
fighting in itself, be it offensive or defensive,
is, as Quakers rightly testify, brutal and
wrong, we can still say with Lessing, "We
know from what failings our virtue springs." [1]
"Sneaks" and "cowards" are epithets of the
worst opprobrium to healthy, simple natures.
Childhood begins life with these notions,
and knighthood also; but, as life grows
larger and its relations many-sided, the early
faith seeks sanction from higher authority
and more rational sources for its own justification, satisfaction, and development. If

[1] Ruskin was one of the most gentle-hearted and
peace-loving men that ever lived. Yet he believed
in war with all the fervor of a worshipper of the
strenuous life. "When I tell you," he says in the
Crown of Wild Olive, "that war is the foundation of
all the arts, I mean also that it is the foundation of
all the high virtues and faculties of men. It is very
strange to me to discover this, and very dreadful,
but I saw it to be quite an undeniable fact. . . .
I found, in brief, that all great nations learned their
truth of word and strength of thought in war; that
they were nourished in war and wasted by peace;
taught by war and deceived by peace; trained by
war and betrayed by peace; in a word, that they
were born in war and expired in peace."

military systems had operated alone, without higher moral support, how far short of chivalry would the ideal of knighthood have fallen! In Europe, Christianity, interpreted with concessions convenient to chivalry, infused it nevertheless with spiritual data. "Religion, war, and glory were the three souls of a perfect Christian knight," says Lamartine. In Japan there were several sources of Bushido.

CHAPTER II

SOURCES OF BUSHIDO

I MAY begin with Buddhism. It furnished a sense of calm trust in Fate, a quiet submission to the inevitable, that stoic composure in sight of danger or calamity, that disdain of life and friendliness with death. A foremost teacher of swordsmanship, when he saw his pupil master the utmost of his art, told him, "Beyond this my instruction must give way to Zen teaching." "Zen" is the Japanese equivalent for the Dhyâna, which "represents human effort to reach through meditation zones of thought beyond the range of verbal expression." [1] Its method is contemplation, and its purport, so far as I understand it, to be convinced of a principle that underlies all phenomena, and, if it can, of the

[1] Lafcadio Hearn, *Exotics and Retrospectives*, p. 84.

Absolute itself, and thus to put oneself in harmony with this Absolute. Thus defined, the teaching was more than the dogma of a sect, and whoever attains to the perception of the Absolute raises himself above mundane things and awakes "to a new Heaven and a new Earth."

What Buddhism failed to give, Shintoism offered in abundance. Such loyalty to the sovereign, such reverence for ancestral memory, and such filial piety as are not taught by any other creed, were inculcated by the Shinto doctrines, imparting passivity to the otherwise arrogant character of the samurai. Shinto theology has no place for the dogma of "original sin." On the contrary, it believes in the innate goodness and Godlike purity of the human soul, adoring it as the adytum from which divine oracles are proclaimed. Everybody has observed that the Shinto shrines are conspicuously devoid of objects and instruments of worship, and that a plain mirror hung in the sanctuary forms the essential part of its furnishing. The presence of this article is easy to explain: it typifies the human heart, which, when perfectly placid and clear, reflects the very image of the Deity. When you stand, therefore, in front of the shrine to worship, you see your own image reflected on its shining surface, and the act of worship is tantamount to the old Delphic injunction, "Know Thyself ." But self-knowledge does not imply, either in the Greek or Japanese teaching, knowledge of the physical part of man, not his anatomy or his psycho-physics; knowledge was to be of a moral kind, the introspection of our moral nature. Mommsen, comparing the Greek and the Roman, says that when the former worshipped he raised his eyes to Heaven, for his prayer was contemplation, while the latter veiled his head, for his was reflection. Essentially like the Roman conception of religion, our reflection brought into prominence not so much the moral as the national consciousness of the individual. Its nature-worship endeared the country to our inmost souls, while its ancestor-worship, tracing from lineage to lineage, made the Imperial family the fountain-head of the whole nation. To us the country is more than land and soil from which to mine gold or to reap grain—it is the sacred abode of the gods, the spirits of our forefathers: to us the Emperor is more than the Arch Constable of a *Rechtsstaat*, or even the Patron of a *Culturstaat*—he is the bodily representative of Heaven on earth, blending in his person its power and its mercy. If what M. Boutmy [1] says is true of English royalty—that it "is not only the image of authority, but the author and symbol of national unity," as I believe it to be, doubly and trebly may this be affirmed of royalty in Japan.

The tenets of Shintoism cover the two predominating features of the emotional life of our race.—Patriotism and Loyalty. Arthur May Knapp very truly says: "In Hebrew literature it is often difficult to tell whether the writer is speaking of God or of the Commonwealth; of Heaven or of Jerusalem; of

[1] *The English People*, p. 188.

the Messiah or of the Nation itself." [1]   A similar confusion may be noticed in the nomenclature of our national faith. I said confusion, because it will be so deemed by a logical intellect on account of its verbal ambiguity; still, being a frame work of national instinct and race feelings, it never pretends to systematic philosophy or a rational theology. This religion—or, is it not more correct to say, the race emotions which this religion expressed?—thoroughly imbued Bushido with loyalty to the sovereign and love of country. These acted more as impulses than as doctrines; for Shintoism, unlike the Mediæval Christian Church, prescribed to its votaries scarcely any *credenda*, furnishing them at the same time with *agenda* of a straightforward and simple type.

As to strictly ethical doctrines, the teachings of Confucius were the most prolific source of Bushido. His enunciation of the five moral relations between master and servant (the governing and the governed), father and

[1] *Feudal and Modern Japan*, vol. i., p. 183.

son, husband and wife, older and younger
brother, and between friend and friend, was
but a confirmation of what the race instinct
had recognised before his writings were introduced from China. The calm, benignant
and worldly-wise character of his politico-
ethical precepts was particularly well suited
to the samurai, who formed the ruling class.
His aristocratic and conservative tone was
well adapted to the requirements of these
warrior statesmen. Next to Confucius, Mencius exercised an immense authority over
Bushido. His forcible and often quite democratic theories were exceedingly taking to
sympathetic natures, and they were even
thought dangerous to, and subversive of, the
existing social order, hence his works were
for a long time under censure. Still, the
words of this master mind found permanent
lodgment in the heart of the samurai.

The writings of Confucius and Mencius
formed the principal text-books for youths
and the highest authority in discussion among
the old. A mere acquaintance with the

classics of these two sages was held, however, in no high esteem. A common proverb ridicules one who has only an intellectual knowledge of Confucius, as a man ever studious but ignorant of *Analects*. A typical samurai calls a literary savant a book-smelling sot. Another compares learning to an ill-smelling vegetable that must be boiled and boiled before it is fit for use. A man who has read little smells a little pedantic, and a man who has read much smells yet more so; both are alike unpleasant. The writer meant thereby that knowledge becomes really such only when it is assimilated in the mind of the learner and shows in his character. An intellectual specialist was considered a machine. Intellect itself was considered subordinate to ethical emotion. Man and the universe were conceived to be alike spiritual and ethical. Bushido could not accept the judgment of Huxley, that the cosmic process was unmoral.

Bushido made light of knowledge of such. It was not pursued as an end in itself, but as a

means to the attainment of wisdom.   Hence,
he who stopped short of this end was regarded
no higher than a convenient machine, which
could turn out poems and maxims at bidding.
Thus, knowledge was conceived as identical
with its practical application in life; and this
Socratic doctrine found its greatest exponent
in the Chinese philosopher, Wan Yang Ming,
who never wearies of repeating, "To know
and to act are one and the same."

I beg leave for a moment's digression while
I am on this subject, inasmuch as some of the
noblest types of *bushi* were strongly influenced
by the teachings of this sage.   Western
readers will easily recognise in his writings
many parallels to the New Testament.
Making allowance for the terms peculiar to
either teaching, the passage, "Seek ye first
the kingdom of God and his righteousness;
and all these things shall be added unto you,"
conveys a thought that may be found on
almost any page of Wan Yang Ming.   A
Japanese disciple [1] of his says—"The lord of

---

[1] Miwa Shissai.

heaven and earth, of all living beings, dwelling in the heart of man, becomes his mind (*Kokoro*); hence a mind is a living thing, and is ever luminous": and again, "The spiritual light of our essential being is pure, and is not affected by the will of man. Spontaneously springing up in our mind, it shows what is right and wrong: it is then called conscience; it is even the light that proceedeth from the god of heaven." How very much do these words sound like some passages from Isaac Pennington or other philosophic mystics! I am inclined to think that the Japanese mind, as expressed in the simple tenets of the Shinto religion, was particularly open to the reception of Yang Ming's precepts. He carried his doctrine of the infallibility of conscience to extreme transcendentalism, attributing to it the faculty to perceive, not only the distinction between right and wrong, but also the nature of psychical facts and physical phenomena. He went as far as, if not farther than, Berkeley and Fichte, in Idealism, denying the existence of things outside of human

ken. If his system had all the logical errors
charged to Solipsism, it had all the efficacy
of strong conviction, and its moral import in
developing individuality of character and
equanimity of temper cannot be gainsaid.

Thus, whatever the sources, the essential
principles which *Bushido* imbibed from them
and assimilated to itself, were few and simple.
Few and simple as these were, they were
sufficient to furnish a safe conduct of life even
through the unsafest days of the most un-
settled period of our nation's history. The
wholesome unsophisticated nature of our
warrior ancestors derived ample food for their
spirit from a sheaf of commonplace and
fragmentary teachings, gleaned as it were on
the highways and byways of ancient thought,
and, stimulated by the demands of the age,
formed from these gleanings a new and
unique type of manhood. An acute French
savant, M. de la Mazelière, thus sums up
his impressions of the sixteenth century:
"Toward the middle of the sixteenth century,
all is confusion in Japan, in the government,

in society, in the church. But the civil wars
the manners returning to barbarism, the
necessity for each to execute justice for himself,—these formed men comparable to those
Italians of the sixteenth century, in whom
Taine praises 'the vigorous initiative, the
habit of sudden resolutions and desperate
undertakings, the grand capacity to do and to
suffer.' In Japan as in Italy 'the rude manners of the Middle Ages' made of man a
superb animal,' wholly militant and wholly
resistant.' And this is why the sixteenth
century displays in the highest degree the
principal quality of the Japanese race, that
great diversity which one finds there between
minds (*esprits*) as well as between tempera-
ments. While in India and even in China
men seem to differ chiefly in degree of energy or intelligence, in Japan they differ by
originality of character as well. Now, individuality is the sign of superior races and of
civilisations already developed. If we make
use of an expression dear to Nietzsche, we
might say that in Asia, to speak of humanity

is to speak of its plains; in Japan as in Europe, one represents it above all by its mountains."

To the pervading characteristics of the men of whom M. de la Mazelière writes, let us now address ourselves. I shall begin with Rectitude.

CHAPTER III

HERE we discern the most cogent precept in the code of the samurai. Nothing is more loathsome to him than underhand dealings and crooked undertakings. The conception of Rectitude may be erroneous—it may be narrow. A well-known bushi defines it as a power of resolution;—"Rectitude is the power of deciding upon a certain course of conduct in accordance with reason, without wavering;—to die when it is right to die, to strike when to strike is right." Another speaks of it in the following terms: "Rectitude is the bone that gives firmness and stature. As without bones the head cannot rest on the top of the spine, nor hands move nor feet stand, so without rectitude neither talent nor learning can make of a human frame a samurai. With it the lack of accomplishments is as nothing." Mencius calls Benevolence man's mind, and Rectitude or Righteousness his path. "How lamentable," he exclaims, "is it to neglect the path and not pursue it, to lose the mind and not know to seek it again! When men's fowls and dogs are lost, they know to seek for them again, but they lose their mind and do not know to seek for it." Have we not here "as in a glass darkly" a parable propounded three hundred years later in another clime and by a greater Teacher, Who called Himself *the* Way of righteousness, through whom the lost could be found? But I stray from my point. Righteousness, according to Mencius, is a straight and narrow path which a man ought to take to regain the lost paradise.

Even in the latter days of feudalism, when the long continuance of peace brought leisure into the life of the warrior class, and with it dissipations of all kinds and accomplishments of gentle arts, the epithet *Gishi* (a man of rectitude) was considered superior to any

name that signified mastery of learning or art.
The Forty-seven Faithfuls—of whom so much
is made in our popular education—are known
in common parlance as the Forty-seven *Gishi*.

In times when cunning artifice was liable to
pass for military tact and downright falsehood
for *ruse de guerre*, this manly virtue, frank
and honest, was a jewel that shone the
brightest and was most highly praised.
Rectitude is a twin brother to Valour, another
martial virtue. But before proceeding to
speak of Valour, let me linger a little while on
what I may term a derivation from Rectitude,
which, at first deviating slightly from its
original, became more and more removed
from it, until its meaning was perverted in the
popular acceptance. I speak of *Gi-ri*, literally the Right Reason, but which came in
time to mean a vague sense of duty which
public opinion expects an incumbent to fulfil.
In its original and unalloyed sense, it meant
duty, pure and simple,—hence, we speak of
the *Giri* we owe to parents, to superiors, to in-
feriors, to society at large, and so forth. In

these instances *Giri* is duty; for what else is duty than what Right Reason demands and commands us to do? Should not Right Reason be our categorical imperative?

Giri primarily meant no more than duty, and I dare say its etymology was derived from the fact, that in our conduct, say to our parents, though love should be the only motive, lacking that, there must be some other authority to enforce filial piety; and they formulated this authority in *Giri*. Very rightly did they formulate this authority —*Giri*—since if love does not rush to deeds of virtue, recourse must be had to man's intellect and his reason must be quickened to convince him of the necessity of acting aright. The same is true of any other moral obligation. The instant Duty becomes onerous, Right Reason steps in to prevent our shirking it. *Giri* thus understood is a severe task-master, with a birch-rod in his hand to make sluggards perform their part. It is a second-ary power in ethics; as a motive it is infinitely inferior to the Christian doctrine of love,

which should be *the* law. I deem it a product
of the conditions of an artificial society—of
a society in which accident of birth and
unmerited favour instituted class distinctions,
in which the family was the social unit, in
which seniority of age was of more account
than superiority of talents, in which natural
affections had often to succumb before
arbitrary man-made customs. Because of
this very artificiality, *Giri* in time degenerated
into a vague sense of propriety called up to
explain this and sanction that,—as, for
example, why a mother must, if need be,
sacrifice all her other children in order to
save the first-born; or why a daughter must
sell her chastity to get funds to pay for the
father's dissipation, and the like. Starting
as Right Reason, *Giri* has, in my opinion,
often stooped to casuistry. It has even
degenerated into cowardly fear of censure. I
might say of *Giri* what Scott wrote of patriotism, that "as it is the fairest, so it is often
the most suspicious, mask of other feelings."
Carried beyond or below Right Reason, *Giri*

became a monstrous misnomer. It harboured under its wings every sort of sophistry and hypocrisy. It would have been easily turned into a nest of cowardice, if Bushido had not a keen and correct sense of courage, the spirit of daring and bearing.

CHAPTER IV

COURAGE, THE SPIRIT OF DARING AND BEARING

COURAGE was scarcely deemed worthy to be counted among virtues, unless it was exercised in the cause of Righteousness. In his *Analects* Confucius defines Courage by explaining, as is often his wont, what its negative is. "Perceiving what is right," he says, "and doing it not, argues lack of courage." Put this epigram into a positive statement, and it runs, "Courage is doing what is right." To run all kinds of hazards, to jeopard one's self, to rush into the jaws of death—these are too often identified with Valour, and in the profession of arms such rashness of conduct—what Shakespeare calls "valour misbegot"—is unjustly applauded; but not so in the Precepts of Knighthood. Death for a cause unworthy of dying for, was called a "dog's death." "To rush into the thick of battle and to be slain in it," says a Prince of Mito, "is easy enough, and the merest churl is equal to the task; but," he continues, "it is true courage to live when it is right to live, and to die only when it is right to die"—and yet the prince had not even heard of the name of Plato, who defines courage as "the knowledge of things that a man should fear and that he should not fear." A distinction which is made in the West between moral and physical courage has long been recognised among us. What samurai youth has not heard of "Great Valour" and the "Valour of a Villain?"

Valour, Fortitude, Bravery, Fearlessness, Courage, being the qualities of soul which appeal most easily to juvenile minds, and which can be trained by exercise and example, were, so to speak, the most popular virtues, early emulated among the youth. Stories of military exploits were repeated almost before boys left their mother's breast. Does a little booby cry for any ache? The mother scolds

him in this fashion: "What a coward to cry
for a trifling pain! What will you do when
your arm is cut off in battle? What when
you are called upon to commit *hara-kiri?*"
We all know the pathetic fortitude of a
famished little boy-prince of Sendai, who in
the drama is made to say to his little page,
"Seest thou those tiny sparrows in the nest,
how their yellow bills are opened wide, and
now see! there comes their mother with worms
to feed them. How eagerly and happily the
little ones eat! but for a samurai, when his
stomach is empty, it is a disgrace to feel
hungry." Anecdotes of fortitude and bravery
abound in nursery tales, though stories of
this kind are not by any means the only
method of early imbuing the spirit with daring and fearlessness. Parents, with sternness
sometimes verging on cruelty, set their
children to tasks that called forth all the
pluck that was in them. "Bears hurl their
cubs down the gorge," they said. Samurai's
sons were let down to steep valleys of hard-
ship, and spurred to Sisyphus-like tasks.

Occasional deprivation of food or exposure to cold, was considered a highly efficacious test for inuring them to endurance. Children of tender age were sent among utter strangers with some message to deliver, were made to rise before the sun, and before breakfast attend to their reading exercises, walking to their teachers with bare feet in the cold of winter; they frequently—once or twice a month, as on the festival of a god of learning, —came together in small groups and passed the night without sleep, in reading aloud by turns. Pilgrimages to all sorts of uncanny places—to execution grounds, to graveyards, to houses reputed of being haunted, were favourite pastimes of the young. In the days when decapitation was public, not only were small boys sent to witness the ghastly scene, but they were made to visit alone the place in the darkness of night and there to leave a mark of their visit on the trunkless head.

Does this ultra-Spartan system [1] of "drilling

[1] The spiritual aspect of valour is evidenced by composure—calm presence of mind. Tranquillity

the nerves" strike the modern pedagogist
with horror and doubt—doubt whether the

is courage in repose. It is a statical manifestation
of valour, as daring deeds are a dynamical. A truly
brave man is ever serene; he is never taken by sur-
prise; nothing ruffles the equanimity of his spirit.
In the heat of battle he remains cool; in the midst
of catastrophes he keeps level his mind. Earth-
quakes do not shake him, he laughs at storms. We
admire him as truly great, who, in the menacing
presence of danger or death, retains his self-posses-
sion; who, for instance, can compose a poem under
impending peril, or hum a strain in the face of death.
Such indulgence betraying no tremor in the writing
or in the voice is taken as an infallible index of a
large nature—of what we call a capacious mind
(*yoyu*), which, far from being pressed or crowded,
has always room for something more.

It passes current among us as a piece of authentic
history, that as Ota Dokan, the great builder of the
castle of Tokyo, was pierced through with a spear,
his assassin, knowing the poetical predilection of his
victim, accompanied his thrust with this couplet:

> "Ah! how in moments like these
> Our heart doth grudge the light of life";

whereupon the expiring hero, not one whit daunted
by the mortal wound in his side, added the lines:

> "Had not in hours of peace,
> It learned to lightly look on life."

There is even a sportive element in a courageous

tendency would not be brutalising, nipping in the bud the tender emotions of the heart?

nature. Things which are serious to ordinary people, may be but play to the valiant. Hence in old warfare it was not at all rare for the parties to a conflict to exchange repartee or to begin a rhetorical contest. Combat was not solely a matter of brute force; it was, as well, an intellectual engagement.

Of such character was the battle fought on the banks of the Koromo River, late in the eleventh century. The eastern army routed, its leader, Sadato, took to flight. When the pursuing general pressed him hard and called aloud, "It is a disgrace for a warrior to show his back to the enemy," Sadato reined his horse; upon this the conquering chief shouted an impromptu verse:

"Torn into shreds is the warp of the cloth" (*koromo*).

Scarcely had the words escaped his lips when the defeated warrior, undismayed, completed the couplet:

"Since age has worn its threads by use."

Yoshiie, whose bow had all the while been bent, suddenly unstrung it and turned away, leaving his prospective victim to do as he pleased. When asked the reason of his strange behaviour, he replied that he could not bear to put to shame one who had kept his presence of mind while hotly pursued by his enemy.

The sorrow which overtook Antony and Octavius at the death of Brutus, has been the general experi-

Let us see in another chapter what other concepts Bushido had of Valour.

ence of brave men. Kenshin, who fought for fourteen years with Shingen, when he heard of the latter's death, wept aloud at the loss of "the best of enemies." It was this same Kenshin who had set a noble example for all time in his treatment of Shingen, whose provinces lay in a mountainous region quite away from the sea, and who had consequently depended upon the Hōjō provinces of the Tokaido for salt. The Hōjō prince wishing to weaken him, although not openly at war with him, had cut off from Shingen all traffic in this important article. Kenshin, hearing of his enemy's dilemma and able to obtain his salt from the coast of his own dominions, wrote Shingen that in his opinion the Hōjō lord had committed a very mean act, and that although he (Kenshin) was at war with him (Shingen) he had ordered his subjects to furnish him with plenty of salt—adding, "I do not fight with salt, but with the sword," affording more than a parallel to the words of Camillus, "We Romans do not fight with gold, but with iron." Nietzsche spoke for the Samurai heart when he wrote, "You are to be proud of your enemy; then the success of your enemy is your success also." Indeed, valour and honour alike required that we should own as enemies in war only such as prove worthy of being friends in peace. When valour attains this height, it becomes akin to Benevolence.

CHAPTER V

LOVE, magnanimity, affection for others, sympathy and pity, were ever recognised to be supreme virtues, the highest of all the attributes of the human soul. It was deemed a princely virtue in a twofold sense: princely among the manifold attributes of a noble spirit; princely as particularly befitting a princely profession. We needed no Shakespeare to feel—though, perhaps, like the rest of the world, we needed him to express it—that mercy became a monarch better than his crown, that it was above his sceptered sway. How often both Confucius and Mencius repeat the highest requirement of a ruler of men to consist in benevolence. Confucius would say,—"Let but a prince cultivate virtue, people will flock to him; with people will come to him lands; lands will bring forth for him wealth; wealth will give him the benefit of right uses. Virtue is the root, and wealth an outcome." Again, "Never has there been a case of a sovereign loving benevolence, and the people not loving righteousness." Mencius follows close at his heels and says, "Instances are on record where individuals attained to supreme power in a single state, without benevolence, but never have I heard of a whole empire falling into the hands of one who lacked this virtue. Also,—It is impossible that any one should become ruler of the people to whom they have not yielded the subjection of their hearts. Both defined this indispensable requirement in a ruler by saying, "Benevolence —benevolence is Man."

Under the regime of feudalism, which could easily degenerate into militarism it was to benevolence that we owed our deliverance from despotism of the worst kind. An utter surrender of "life and limb" on the part of the governed would have left nothing for the governing but self-will, and this has for its natural consequence the growth of that absolutism so often called "oriental despotism," as though there were no despots of occidental history!

Let it be far from me to uphold despotism of any sort; but it is a mistake to identify feudalism with it. When Frederick the Great wrote that "Kings are the first servants of the State," jurists thought rightly that a new era was reached in the development of freedom. Strangely coinciding in time, in the backwoods of North-western Japan, Yozan of Yonézawa made exactly the same declaration, showing that feudalism was not all tyranny and oppression. A feudal prince, although unmindful of owing reciprocal obligations to his vassals, felt a higher sense of responsibility to his ancestors and to Heaven. He was a father to his subjects, whom Heaven entrusted to his care. According to the ancient Chinese *Book of Poetry*, "Until the house of Yin lost the hearts of the people, they could appear before Heaven." And

Confucius in his *Great Learning* taught:
"When the prince loves what the people
love and hates what the people hate, then
is he what is called the parent of the people." Thus are public opinion and monarchical will or democracy and absolutism
merged one in the other. Thus also, in a sense
not usually assigned to the term, Bushido
accepted and corroborated paternal government—paternal also as opposed to the less
interested avuncular government. (Uncle
Sam's, to wit!) The difference between a
despotic and a paternal government lies in
this, that in the one the people obey re-
luctantly, while in the other they do so with
"that proud submission, that dignified obedience, that subordination of heart which kept
alive, even in servitude itself, the spirit of
exalted freedom." [1] The old saying is not
entirely false which called the king of England the "king of devils, because of his
subjects' often insurrections against, and de-
positions of, their princes," and which made

[1] Burke, *French Revolution.*

the French monarch the "king of asses,"
because of their infinite taxes and imposi-
tions," but which gave the title of the king of
men to the sovereign of Spain "because of his
subjects' willing obedience." But enough!

Virtue and absolute power may strike the
Anglo-Saxon mind as terms which it is
impossible to harmonise. Pobyedonostseff
has clearly set forth before us the contrast in
the foundations of English and other European communities; namely, that these were
organised on the basis of common interest,
while that was distinguished by a strongly
developed independent personality. What
this Russian statesman says of the personal
dependence of individuals on some social
alliance and in the end of ends on the State,
among the continental nations of Europe and
particularly among Slavonic peoples, is doubly
true of the Japanese. Hence not only is a
free exercise of monarchical power not felt
as heavily by us as in Europe, but it is
generally moderated by paternal consideration for the feelings of the people. "Absolut-

ism," says Bismarck, "primarily demands
in the ruler impartiality, honesty, devotion to
duty, energy and inward humility." If I
may be allowed to make one more quotation
on this subject, I will cite from the speech of
the German Emperor at Coblenz, in which he
spoke of "Kingship, by the grace of God,
with its heavy duties, its tremendous responsibilities to the Creator alone, from
which no man, no minister, no parliament,
can release the monarch."

We knew benevolence was a tender virtue
and mother-like. If upright Rectitude and
stern Justice were peculiarly masculine,
Mercy had the gentleness and the persuasive-
ness of a feminine nature. We were warned
against indulging in indiscriminate charity,
without seasoning it with justice and rectitude. Masamuné expressed it well in his
oft-quoted aphorism—"Rectitude carried to
excess hardens into stiffness; benevolence in-
dulged beyond measure sinks into weakness."

Fortunately mercy was not so rare as it was
beautiful, for it is universally true that "The

bravest are the tenderest, the loving are the daring." "*Bushi no nasaké*"—the tenderness of a warrior—had a sound which appealed at once to whatever was noble in us; not that the mercy of a samurai was generically different from the mercy of any other being, but because it implied mercy where mercy was not a blind impulse, but where it recognised due regard to justice, and where mercy did not remain merely a certain state of mind, but where it was backed with power to save or kill. As economists speak of demand as being effectual or ineffectual, similarly we may call the mercy of Bushi effectual, since it implied the power of acting for the good or detriment of the recipient.

Priding themselves as they did in their brute strength and privileges to turn it into account, the samurai gave full consent to what Mencius taught concerning the power of love. "Benevolence," he says, "brings under its sway whatever hinders its power, just as water subdues fire: they only doubt the power of water to quench flames who try to extinguish with a cupful a whole burning waggon-load of fagots." He also says that "the feeling of distress is the root of benevolence," therefore a benevolent man is ever mindful of those who are suffering and in distress. Thus did Mencius long anticipate Adam Smith who founds his ethical philosophy on sympathy.

It is indeed striking how closely the code of knightly honour of one country coincides with that of others; in other words, how the much-abused oriental ideas of morals find their counterparts in the noblest maxims of European literature. If the well-known lines,

> Hæ tibi erunt artes—pacisque imponere morem,
> Parcere subjectis, et debellare superbos,

were shown a Japanese gentleman, he might readily accuse the Mantuan bard of plagiarising from the literature of his own country.

Benevolence to the weak, the down-trodden or the vanquished, was ever extolled as peculiarly becoming to a samurai. Lovers of Japanese art must be familiar with the representation of a priest riding backwards on a cow. The rider was once a warrior who in his day made his name a by-word of terror. In that terrible battle of Sumano - ura, (1184 A.D.) which was one of the most decisive in our history, he overtook an enemy and in single combat had him in the clutch of his gigantic arms. Now the etiquette of war required that on such occasions no blood should be spilt, unless the weaker party proved to be a man of rank or ability equal to that of the stronger. The grim combatant would have the name of the man under him; but he refusing to make it known, his helmet was ruthlessly torn off, when the sight of a juvenile face, fair and beardless, made the astonished knight relax his hold. Helping the youth to his feet, in paternal tones he bade the stripling go: "Off, young prince, to thy mother's side! The sword of Kumagayé shall never be tarnished by a drop of thy blood. Haste and flee o'er yon pass before thine enemies come in sight!" The young warrior refused to go and begged Kumagayé, for the honour of both, to dispatch him on the spot. Above the hoary head of the veteran gleams the cold blade, which many a time before has sundered the chords of life, but his stout heart quails; there flashes athwart his mental eye the vision of his own boy, who this self-same day marched to the sound of bugle to try his maiden arms; the strong hand of the warrior quivers; again he begs his victim to flee for his life. Finding all his entreaties vain and hearing the approaching steps of his comrades, he exclaims: "If thou art over-taken, thou mayst fall at a more ignoble hand than mine. O thou Infinite! receive his soul!" In an instant the sword flashes in the air, and when it falls it is red with adolescent blood. When the war is ended, we find our soldier returning in triumph, but little cares he now for honour or fame; he renounces his warlike career, shaves his head, dons a priestly garb, devotes the rest of his days to holy pilgrimage, never turning his back to the West where lies the Paradise whence salvation comes and whither the sun hastes daily for his rest.

Critics may point out flaws in this story, which is casuistically vulnerable. Let it be: all the same it shows that Tenderness, Pity, and Love were traits which adorned the most sanguinary exploits of a samurai. It was an old maxim among them that "It becometh not the fowler to slay the bird which takes refuge in his bosom." This in a large measure explains why the Red Cross movement, considered so peculiarly Christian, so readily found a firm footing among us. Decades before we heard of the Geneva Convention, Bakin, our greatest novelist, had familiarised us with the medical treatment of a fallen foe. In the principality of Satsuma, noted for its martial spirit and education, the custom prevailed for young men to practise music; not the blast of trumpets or the beat of drums,—"those clamorous harbingers of blood and death"—stirring us to imitate the actions of a tiger, but sad and tender melodies on the *biwa*,[1] soothing our fiery spirits, drawing our thoughts away from

[1] A musical instrument, resembling the guitar.

scent of blood and scenes of carnage. Polybius tells us of the Constitution of Arcadia, which required all youths under thirty to practise music, in order that this gentle art might alleviate the rigours of the inclement region. It is to its influence that he attributes the absence of cruelty in that part of the Arcadian mountains.

Nor was Satsuma the only place in Japan where gentleness was inculcated among the warrior class. A Prince of Shirakawa jots down his random thoughts, and among them is the following: "Though they come stealing to your bedside in the silent watches of the night, drive not away, but rather cherish these—the fragrance of flowers, the sound of distant bells, the insect hummings of a frosty night." And again, "Though they may wound your feelings, these three you have only to forgive, the breeze that scatters your flowers, the cloud that hides your moon, and the man who tries to pick quarrels with you."

It was ostensibly to express, but actually to cultivate, these gentler emotions that the writing of verses was encouraged. Our poetry has therefore a strong undercurrent of pathos and tenderness. A well-known anecdote of a rustic samurai illustrates the case in point. When he was told to learn versification, and "The Warbler's Notes"[1] was given him for the subject of his first attempt, his fiery spirit rebelled and he flung at the feet of his master this uncouth production, which ran

> "The brave warrior keeps apart
> The ear that might listen
> To the warbler's song."

His master, undaunted by the crude sentiment, continued to encourage the youth, until one day the music of his soul was awakened to respond to the sweet notes of the *uguisu*, and he wrote

> "Stands the warrior, mailed and strong,
> To hear the uguisu's song,
> Warbled sweet the trees among."

We admire and enjoy the heroic incident in Körner's short life, when, as he lay wounded

[1] The uguisu or warbler, sometimes called the nightingale of Japan.

on the battle-field, he scribbled his famous
Farewell to Life. Incidents of a similar
kind were not at all unusual in our warfare.
Our pithy, epigrammatic poems were particularly well suited to the improvisation of a
single sentiment. Everybody of any education was either a poet or a poetaster. Not
infrequently a marching soldier might be seen
to halt, take his writing utensils from his belt,
and compose an ode,—and such papers were
found afterward in the helmets or the breast-
plates when these were removed from their
lifeless wearers.

What Christianity has done in Europe
toward rousing compassion in the midst of
belligerent horrors, love of music and letters
has done in Japan. The cultivation of tender
feelings breeds considerate regard for the
sufferings of others. Modesty and com-
plaisance, actuated by respect for others'
feelings, are at the root of politeness.

CHAPTER VI

COURTESY and urbanity of manners have been noticed by every foreign tourist as a marked Japanese trait. Politeness is a poor virtue, if it is actuated only by a fear of offending good taste, whereas it should be the outward manifestation of a sympathetic regard for the feelings of others. It also implies a due regard for the fitness of things, therefore due respect to social positions; for these latter express no plutocratic distinctions, but were originally distinctions for actual merit.

In its highest form, politeness almost approaches love. We may reverently say, politeness "suffereth long, and is kind; envieth not, vaunteth not itself, is not puffed up; doth not behave itself unseemly, seeketh

50

not her own, is not easily provoked, taketh not account of evil." Is it any wonder that Professor Dean, in speaking of the six elements of humanity, accords to politeness an exalted position, inasmuch as it is the ripest fruit of social intercourse?

While thus extolling politeness, far be it from me to put it in the front rank of virtues. If we analyse it, we shall find it correlated with other virtues of a higher order; for what virtue stands alone? While—or rather because—it was exalted as peculiar to the profession of arms, and as such esteemed in a degree higher than its deserts, there came into existence its counterfeits. Confucius himself has repeatedly taught that external appurtenances are as little a part of propriety as sounds are of music.

When propriety was elevated to the *sine qua non* of social intercourse, it was only to be expected that an elaborate system of etiquette should come into vogue to train youth in correct social behaviour. How one must bow in accosting others, how he must walk and sit, were taught and learned with utmost care. Table manners grew to be a science. Tea serving and drinking were raised to ceremony. A man of education is, of course, expected to be master of all these. Very fitly does Mr. Veblen, in his interesting book,[1] call decorum "a product and an exponent of the leisure-class life."

I have heard slighting remarks made by Europeans upon our elaborate discipline of politeness. It has been criticised as absorbing too much of our thought and in so far a folly to observe strict obedience to it. I admit that there may be unnecessary niceties in ceremonious etiquette, but whether it partakes as much of folly as the adherence to ever-changing fashions of the West, is a question not very clear to my mind. Even fashions I do not consider solely as freaks of vanity; on the contrary, I look upon these as a ceaseless search of the human mind for the beautiful. Much less do I consider elaborate ceremony as altogether trivial; for it denotes

[1] *Theory of the Leisure Class*, N. Y., 1899, p. 46.

the result of long observation as to the most
appropriate method of achieving a certain
result. If there is anything to do, there is
certainly a best way to do it, and the best way
is both the most economical and the most
graceful. Mr. Spencer defines grace as the
most economical manner of motion. The tea
ceremony presents certain definite ways of
manipulating a bowl, a spoon, a napkin, etc.
To a novice it looks tedious. But one soon
discovers that the way prescribed is, after all,
the most saving of time and labour; in other
words, the most economical use of force,—
hence, according to Spencer's dictum, the
most graceful.

The spiritual significance of social decorum
—or, I might say, to borrow from the vocabulary of the "Philosophy of Clothes," the
spiritual discipline of which etiquette and
ceremony are mere outward garments — is
out of all proportion to what their appearance
warrants us in believing. I might follow the
example of Mr. Spencer and trace in our
ceremonial institutions their origins and the

moral motives that gave rise to them; but that is not what I shall endeavour to do in this book. It is the moral training involved in strict observance of propriety, that I wish to emphasise.

I have said that etiquette was elaborated into the finest niceties, so much so that different schools, advocating different systems, came into existence. But they all united in the ultimate essential, and this was put by a great exponent of the best known school of etiquette, the Ogasawara, in the following terms: "The end of all etiquette is to so cultivate your mind that even when you are quietly seated, not the roughest ruffian can dare make onset on your person." It means, in other words, that by constant exercise in correct manners, one brings all the parts and faculties of his body into perfect order and into such harmony with itself and its environment as to express the mastery of spirit over the flesh. What a new and deep significance the French word *bienséance*[1] comes to contain.

[1] Etymologically, well-seatedness.

If the promise is true that gracefulness means economy of force, then it follows as a logical sequence that a constant practice of graceful deportment must bring with it a reserve and storage of force. Fine manners, therefore, mean power in repose. When the barbarian Gauls, during the sack of Rome, burst into the assembled Senate and dared pull the beards of the venerable Fathers, we think the old gentlemen were to blame, inasmuch as they lacked dignity and strength of manners. Is lofty spiritual attainment really possible through etiquette? Why not? —All roads lead to Rome!

As an example of how the simplest thing can be made into an art and then become spiritual culture, I may take *Cha-no-yu*, the tea ceremony. Tea-sipping as a fine art! Why should it not be? In the children drawing pictures on the sand, or in the savage carving on a rock, was the promise of a Raphael or a Michael Angelo. How much more is the drinking of a beverage, which began with the transcendental contemplation of a Hindoo anchorite, entitled to develop into a handmaid of Religion and Morality? That calmness of mind, that serenity of temper, that composure and quietness of demeanour which are the first essentials of *Cha-no-yu*, are without doubt the first conditions of right thinking and right feeling. The scrupulous cleanliness of the little room, shut off from sight and sound of the madding crowd, is in itself conducive to direct one's thoughts from the world. The bare interior does not engross one's attention like the innumerable pictures and bric-a-brac of a Western parlour; the presence of *kakémono*[1] calls our attention more to grace of design than to beauty of colour. The utmost refinement of taste is the object aimed at; whereas anything like display is banished with religious horror. The very fact that it was invented by a contemplative recluse, in a time when wars and the rumours of wars were incessant, is well calculated to show that this

[1] Hanging scrolls, which may be either paintings or ideograms, used for decorative purposes.

institution was more than a pastime. Before entering the quiet precincts of the tea-room, the company assembling to partake of the ceremony laid aside, together with their swords, the ferocity of battle-field or the cares of government, there to find peace and friendship.

Cha-no-yu is more than a ceremony—it is a fine art; it is poetry, with articulate gestures for rhythms: it is a *modus operandi* of soul discipline. Its greatest value lies in this last phase. Not infrequently the other phases preponderated in the mind of its votaries. but that does not prove that its essence was not of a spiritual nature.

Politeness will be a great acquisition, if it does no more than impart grace to manners; but its function does not stop here. For propriety, springing as it does from motives of benevolence and modesty, and actuated by tender feelings toward the sensibilities of others, is ever a graceful expression of sympathy. Its requirement is that we should weep with those that weep and rejoice with those that rejoice. Such didactic requirement, when reduced into small everyday details of life, expresses itself in little acts scarcely noticeable, or, if noticed, is, as one missionary lady of twenty years' residence once said to me, "awfully funny." You are out in the hot, glaring sun with no shade over you; a Japanese acquaintance passes by; you accost him, and instantly his hat is off—well, that is perfectly natural, but the "awfully funny" performance is, that all the while he talks with you his parasol is down and he stands in the glaring sun also. How foolish! —Yes, exactly so, provided the motive were less than this: "You are in the sun; I sympathise with you; I would willingly take you under my parasol if it were large enough, or if we were familiarly acquainted; as I cannot shade you, I will share your discomforts." Little acts of this kind, equally or more amusing, are not mere gestures or conventionalities. They are the "bodying forth" of thoughtful feelings for the comfort of others.

Another "awfully funny" custom is dictated by our canons of Politeness; but many

superficial writers on Japan have dismissed it
by simply attributing it to the general topsy-
turvyness of the nation. Every foreigner
who has observed it will confess the awkward-
ness he felt in making proper reply upon the
occasion. In America, when you make a gift,
you sing its praises to the recipient; in Japan
we depreciate or slander it. The underlying
idea with you is, "This is a nice: gift if it
were not nice I would not dare give it to you;
for it will be an insult to give you anything
but what is nice." In contrast to this, our
logic runs: "You are a nice person, and no
gift is nice enough for you. You will not
accept anything I can lay at your feet except
as a token of my good will; so accept this, not
for its intrinsic value, but as a token. It will
be an insult to your worth to call the best
gift good enough for you." Place the two
ideas side by side, and we see that the ultimate idea is one and the same. Neither is
"awfully funny." The American speaks of the
material which makes the gift; the Japanese
speaks of the spirit which prompts the gift

It is perverse reasoning to conclude, because our sense of propriety shows itself in all the smallest ramifications of our deportment, to take the least important of them and uphold it as the type, and pass judgment upon the principle itself. Which is more important, to eat or to observe rules of propriety about eating? A Chinese sage answers, "If you take a case where the eating is all-important, and the observing the rules of propriety is of little importance, and compare them together, why not merely say that the eating is of the more importance?" "Metal is heavier than feathers," but does that saying have reference to a single clasp of metal and a waggon-load of feathers? Take a piece of wood a foot thick and raise it above the pinnacle of a temple, none would call it taller than the temple. To the question, "Which is the more important, to tell the truth or to be polite?" the Japanese are said to give an answer diametrically opposite to what the American will say, —but I forbear any comment until I come to speak of veracity and sincerity.

CHAPTER VII

VERACITY AND SINCERITY

WITHOUT veracity and sincerity, politeness is a farce and a show. "Propriety carried beyond right bounds," says Masamuné, "becomes a lie." An ancient poet has outdone Polonius in the advice he gives: "To thyself be faithful: if in thy heart thou strayest not from truth, without prayer of thine the Gods will keep thee whole." The apotheosis of Sincerity to which Confucius gives expression in the *Doctrine of the Mean*, attributes to it transcendental powers, almost identifying them with the Divine. "Sincerity is the end and the beginning of all things; without Sincerity there would be nothing." He then dwells with eloquence on its far-reaching and long-enduring nature, its power to produce changes without movement and by its mere presence to accomplish its purpose without effort. From the Chinese ideogram for Sincerity, which is a combination of "Word" and "Perfect," one is tempted to draw a parallel between it and the Neo-Platonic doctrine of *Logos*—to such height does the sage soar in his unwonted mystic flight.

Lying or equivocation were deemed equally cowardly. The bushi held that his high social position demanded a loftier standard of veracity than that of the tradesman and peasant. *Bushi no ichi-gon*—the word of a samurai, or in exact German equivalent, *Ritterwort*—was sufficient guaranty for the truthfulness of an assertion. His word carried such weight with it that promises were generally made and fulfilled without a written pledge, which would have been deemed quite beneath his dignity. Many thrilling anecdotes were told of those who atoned by death for *ni-gon*, a double tongue.

The regard for veracity was so high that, unlike the generality of Christians who persistently violate the plain commands of the Teacher not to swear, the best of samurai looked upon an oath as derogatory to their honour. I am well aware that they did swear by different deities or upon their swords; but never has swearing degenerated into wanton form and irreverent interjection. To emphasise our words a practice was sometimes resorted to of literally sealing with blood. For the explanation of such a practice, I need only refer my readers to Goethe's *Faust.*

A recent American writer is responsible for this statement, that if you ask an ordinary Japanese which is better, to tell a falsehood or be impolite, he will not hesitate to answer, "To tell a falsehood!" Dr. Peery [1] is partly right and partly wrong; right in that an ordinary Japanese, even a samurai, may answer in the way ascribed to him, but wrong in attributing too much weight to the term he translates "falsehood." This word (in Japanese, *uso*) is employed to denote anything which is not a truth (*makoto*) or fact (*honto*).

[1] Peery, *The Gist of Japan*, p. 86.

Lowell tells us that Wordsworth could not distinguish between truth and fact, and an ordinary Japanese is in this respect as good as Wordsworth. Ask a Japanese, or even an American of any refinement, to tell you whether he dislikes you or whether he is sick at his stomach, and he will not hesitate long to tell falsehoods and answer "I like you much," or, "I am quite well, thank you." To sacrifice truth merely for the sake of politeness was regarded as an "empty form" (*kyo-rei*) and "deception by sweet words."

I own I am speaking now of the Bushido idea of veracity: but it may not be amiss to devote a few words to our commercial integrity, of which I have heard much complaint in foreign books and journals. A loose business morality has indeed been the worst blot on our national reputation; but before abusing it or hastily condemning the whole race for it, let us calmly study it and we shall be rewarded with consolation for the future.

Of all the great occupations of life, none was farther removed from the profession of arms than commerce. The merchant was placed lowest in the category of vocations,—the knight, the tiller of the soil, the mechanic, the merchant. The samurai derived his income from land and could even indulge, if he had a mind to, in amateur farming; but the counter and abacus were abhorred. We know the wisdom of this social arrangement. Montesquieu has made it clear that the debarring of the nobility from mercantile pursuits was an admirable social policy, in that it prevented wealth from accumulating in the hands of the powerful. The separation of power and riches kept the distribution of the latter more nearly equable. Professor Dill, the author of *Roman Society in the Last Century of the Western Empire*, has brought afresh to our mind that one cause of the decadence of the Roman Empire, was the permission given to the nobility to engage in trade, and the consequent monopoly of wealth and power by a minority of the senatorial families.

Commerce, therefore, in feudal Japan did not reach that degree of development which it would have attained under freer conditions. The obloquy attached to the calling naturally brought within its pale such as cared little for social repute. "Call one a thief and he will steal." Put a stigma on a calling and its followers adjust their morals to it, for it is natural that "the normal conscience," as Hugh Black says, "rises to the demands made on it, and easily falls to the limit of the standard expected from it." It is unnecessary to add that no business, commercial or otherwise, can be transacted without a code of morals. Our merchants of the feudal period had one among themselves, without which they could never have developed, as they did in embryo, such fundamental mercantile institutions as the guild, the bank, the bourse, insurance, checks, bills of exchange, etc.; but in their relations with people outside their vocation, the tradesmen lived too true to the reputation of their order.

This being the case, when the country was opened to foreign trade, only the most adventurous and unscrupulous rushed to the

ports, while the respectable business houses
declined for some time the repeated requests
of the authorities to establish branch houses.
Was Bushido powerless to stay the current of
commercial dishonour? Let us see.

Those who are well acquainted with our
history will remember that only a few years
after our treaty ports were opened to foreign
trade, feudalism was abolished, and when with
it the samurai's fiefs were taken and bonds
issued to them in compensation, they were
given liberty to invest them in mercantile
transactions. Now you may ask, "Why
could they not bring their much boasted
veracity into their new business relations and
so reform the old abuses?" Those who had
eyes to see could not weep enough, those who
had hearts to feel could not sympathise
enough, with the fate of many a noble and
honest samurai who signally and irrevocably
failed in his new and unfamiliar field of trade
and industry, through sheer lack of shrewd-
ness in coping with his artful plebeian rival.
When we know that eighty per cent. of the

business houses fail in so industrial a country as America, is it any wonder that scarcely one among a hundred samurai who went into trade could succeed in his new vocation? It will be long before it will be recognised how many fortunes were wrecked in the attempt to apply Bushido ethics to business methods; but it was soon patent to every observing mind that the ways of wealth were not the ways of honour. In what respects, then, were they different?

Of the three incentives to veracity that Lecky enumerates, viz., the industrial, the political, and the philosophical, the first was altogether lacking in Bushido. As to the second, it could develop little in a political community under a feudal system. It is in its philosophical and, as Lecky says, in its highest aspect, that honesty attained elevated rank in our catalogue of virtues. With all my sincere regard for the high commercial integrity of the Anglo-Saxon race, when I ask for the ultimate ground, I am told that "honesty is the best policy,"—that it *pays* to be honest. Is not this virtue, then, its own reward? If it is followed because it brings in more cash than falsehood, I am afraid Bushido would rather indulge in lies!

If Bushido rejects a doctrine of *quid pro quo* rewards, the shrewder tradesman will readily accept it. Lecky has very truly remarked that veracity owes its growth largely to commerce and manufacture; as Nietzsche puts it, honesty is the youngest of the virtues—in other words, it is the foster-child of modern indust y. Without this mother, veracity was like a blue-blood orphan whom only the most cultivated mind could adopt and nourish. Such minds were general among the samurai, but, for want of a more democratic and utilitarian foster-mother, the tender child failed to thrive. Industries advancing, veracity will prove an easy, nay, a profitable virtue to practise. Just think— as late as November, 1880, Bismarck sent a circular to the professional consuls of the German Empire, warning them of "a lamentable lack of reliability with regard to German shipments *inter alia*, apparent both as to quality and quantity." Nowadays we hear comparatively little of German carelessness and dishonesty in trade. In twenty years her merchants have learned that in the end honesty pays. Already our merchants have found that out. For the rest I recommend the reader to two recent writers for well-weighed judgment on this point.[1] It is interesting to remark in this connection that integrity and honour were the surest guaranties which even a merchant debtor could present in the form of promissory notes. It was quite a usual thing to insert such clauses as these: "In default of the repayment of the sum lent to me, I shall say nothing against being ridiculed in public"; or, "In case I fail to pay you back, you may call me a fool," and the like.

Often have I wondered whether the veracity of Bushido had any motive higher than courage. In the absence of any positive

[1] Knapp, *Feudal and Modern Japan*, Vol. I., ch. iv.; Ransome, *Japan in Transition*, ch. viii.

commandment against bearing false witness, lying was not condemned as sin, but simply denounced as weakness, and, as such, highly dishonourable. As a matter of fact, the idea of honesty is so intimately blended, and its Latin and its German etymology so identified with honour, that it is high time I should pause a few moments for the consideration of this feature of the Precepts of Knighthood.

CHAPTER VIII

HONOUR

THE sense of honour, implying a vivid consciousness of personal dignity and worth, could not fail to characterise the samurai, born and bred to value the duties and privileges of their profession. Though the word ordinarily given nowadays as the translation of honour was not used freely, yet the idea was conveyed by such terms as *na* (name) *men-moku* (countenance), *guai-bun* (outside hearing), reminding us respectively of the biblical use of "name," of the evolution of the term "personality" from the Greek mask, and of "fame." A good name — one's reputation, "the immortal part of one's self, what remains being bestial"—assumed as a matter of course, any infringement upon its integrity

was felt as shame, and the sense of shame
(*Ren-chi-shin*) was one of the earliest to be
cherished in juvenile education. "You will
be laughed at," "It will disgrace you," "Are
you not ashamed?" were the last appeal to
correct behaviour on the part of a youthful
delinquent. Such a recourse to his honour
touched the most sensitive spot in the child's
heart, as though it had been nursed on honour
while he was in his mother's womb; for most
truly is honour a pre-natal influence, being
closely bound up with strong family consciousness. "In losing the solidarity of
families," says Balzac, "society has lost the
fundamental force which Montesquieu named
Honour." Indeed, the sense of shame seems
to me to be the earliest indication of the
moral consciousness of the race. The first
and worst punishment which befell humanity
in consequence of tasting "the fruit of that
forbidden tree" was, to my mind, not the
sorrow of child-birth, nor the thorns and
thistles, but the awakening of the sense of
shame. Few incidents in history excel in

pathos the scene of the first mother plying, with heaving breast and tremulous fingers, her crude needle on the few fig leaves which her dejected husband plucked for her. This first fruit of disobedience clings to us with a tenacity that nothing else does. All the sartorial ingenuity of mankind has not yet succeeded in sewing an apron that will efficaciously hide our sense of shame. That samurai was right who refused to compromise his character by a slight humiliation in his youth; "because," he said, "dishonour is like a scar on a tree, which time, instead of effacing, only helps to enlarge."

Mencius had taught centuries before, in almost the identical phrase, what Carlyle has latterly expressed,—namely, that "Shame is the soil of all Virtue, of good manners and good morals."

The fear of disgrace was so great that if our literature lacks such eloquence as Shakespeare puts into the mouth of Norfolk, it nevertheless hung like Damocles' sword over the head of every samurai and often assumed a morbid character. In the name of honour, deeds were perpetrated which can find no justification in the code of Bushido. At the slightest, nay—imaginary insult—the quick-tempered braggart took offence, resorted to the use of the sword, and many an unnecessary strife was raised and many an innocent life lost. The story of a well-meaning citizen who called the attention of a bushi to a flea jumping on his back, and who was forthwith cut in two, for the simple and questionable reason, that inasmuch as fleas are parasites which feed on animals, it was an unpardonable insult to identify a noble warrior with a beast—I say, stories like these are too frivolous to believe. Yet, the circulation of such stories implies three things: (1) that they were invented to overawe common people; (2) that abuses were really made of the samurai's profession of honour; and (3) that a very strong sense of shame was developed among them. It is plainly unfair to take an abnormal case to cast blame upon the precepts, any more than to judge of the true teachings of Christ from the fruits of religious fanaticism and extravagance,—inquisitions and hypocrisy. But, as in religious monomania there is something touchingly noble as compared with the delirium tremens of a drunkard, so in that extreme sensitiveness of the samurai about their honour do we not recognise the substratum of a genuine virtue?

The morbid excess into which the delicate code of honour was inclined to run was strongly counterbalanced by preaching magnanimity and patience. To take offence at slight provocation was ridiculed as "short-tempered." The popular adage said: "To bear what you think you cannot bear is really to bear." The great Iyéyasu left to posterity a few maxims, among which are the following: —"The life of man is like going a long distance with a heavy load upon the shoulders. Haste not. . . . Reproach none, but be forever watchful of thine own short-comings. . . . Forbearance is the basis of length of days." He proved in his life what he preached. A literary wit put a character-

istic epigram into the mouths of three well-
known personages in our history: to Nobunaga he attributed, "I will kill her, if the
nightingale sings not in time"; to Hidéyoshi,
"I will force her to sing for me"; and to
Iyéyasu, "I will wait till she opens her lips."

Patience and long-suffering were also
highly commended by Mencius. In one
place he writes to this effect: "Though you
denude yourself and insult me, what is that to
me? You cannot defile my soul by your
outrage." Elsewhere he teaches that anger
at a petty offence is unworthy a superior man,
but indignation for a great cause is righteous
wrath.

To what height of unmartial and unresist-
ing meekness Bushido could reach in some of
its votaries, may be seen in their utterances.
Take, for instance, this saying of Ogawa:
"When others speak all manner of evil things
against thee, return not evil for evil, but
rather reflect that thou wast not more faithful in the discharge of thy duties." Take
another of Kumazawa:—"When others blame

thee, blame them not; when others are angry at thee, return not anger. Joy cometh only as Passion and Desire part." Still another instance I may cite from Saigo, upon whose overhanging brows "Shame is ashamed to sit":—"The Way is the way of Heaven and Earth; Man's place is to follow it; therefore make it the object of thy life to reverence Heaven. Heaven loves me and others with equal love; therefore with the love wherewith thou lovest thyself, love others. Make not Man thy partner but Heaven, and making Heaven thy partner do thy best. Never condemn others; but see to it that thou comest not short of thine own mark." Some of these sayings remind us of Christian expostulations, and show us how far in practical morality natural religion can approach the revealed. Not only did these sayings remain as utterances, but they were really embodied in acts.

It must be admitted that very few attained this sublime height of magnanimity, patience and forgiveness. It was a great pity that

nothing clear and general was expressed as to
what constitutes honour, only a few enlightened minds being aware that it "from
no condition rises," but that it lies in each
acting well his part; for nothing was easier
than for youths to forget in the heat of action
what they had learned in Mencius in their
calmer moments. Said this sage: "'T is in
every man's mind to love honour; but little
doth he dream that what is truly honourable
lies within himself and not elsewhere. The
honour which men confer is not good honour.
Those whom Châo the Great ennobles, he can
make mean again." For the most part, an
insult was quickly resented and repaid by
death, as we shall see later, while honour—
too often nothing higher than vainglory or
worldly approbation—was prized as the *sum-
mum bonum* of earthly existence. Fame,
and not wealth or knowledge, was the goal
toward which youths had to strive. Many a
lad swore within himself as he crossed the
threshold of his paternal home, that he would
not recross it until he had made a name in the

world; and many an ambitious mother refused to see her sons again unless they could
"return home," as the expression is, "capari-
soned in brocade." To shun shame or win a
name, samurai boys would submit to any
privations and undergo severest ordeals of
bodily or mental suffering. They knew that
honour won in youth grows with age. In the
memorable seige of Osaka, a young son of
Iyéyasu, in spite of his earnest entreaties to
be put in the vanguard, was placed at the
rear of the army. When the castle fell, he
was so chagrined and wept so bitterly that an
old councillor tried to console him with all the
resources at his command; "Take comfort,
Sire," said he, "at the thought of the long
future before you. In the many years that
you may live, there will come divers occasions
to distinguish yourself." The boy fixed his
indignant gaze upon the man and said—"How
foolishly you talk! Can ever my fourteenth
year come round again?" Life itself was
thought cheap if honour and fame could be
attained therewith: hence, whenever a cause

presented itself which was considered dearer than life, with utmost serenity and celerity was life laid down.

Of the causes in comparison with which no life was too dear to sacrifice, was the duty of loyalty, which was the key-stone making feudal virtues a symmetrical arch.

6

CHAPTER IX

THE DUTY OF LOYALTY

FEUDAL morality shares other virtues in common with other systems of ethics, with other classes of people, but this virtue—homage and fealty to a superior—is its distinctive feature. I am aware that personal fidelity is a moral adhesion existing among all sorts and conditions of men,—a gang of pickpockets owe allegiance to a Fagin; but it is only in the code of chivalrous honour that loyalty assumes paramount importance.

In spite of Hegel's criticism [1] that the fidelity of feudal vassals, being an obligation to an individual and not to a commonwealth, is a bond established on totally unjust principles, a great compatriot of his made it his boast that personal loyalty was a German

[1] *Philosophy of History* (Eng. trans. by Sibree), Pt. IV., sec. ii., ch. i.

virtue. Bismarck had good reasons to do so,
not because the *Treue* he boasts of was the
monopoly of his Fatherland or of any single
nation or race, but because this favoured
fruit of chivalry lingers latest among the
people where feudalism has lasted longest.
In America, where "everybody is as good as
anybody else," and, as the Irishman added,
"better too," such exalted ideas of loyalty as
we feel for our sovereign may be deemed
"excellent within certain bounds," but pre-
posterous as encouraged among us. Montesquieu complained long ago that right on one
side of the Pyrenees was wrong on the other,
and the recent Dreyfus trial proved the truth
of his remark, save that the Pyrenees were
not the sole boundary beyond which French
justice finds no accord. Similarly, loyalty
as we conceive it may find few admirers elsewhere, not because our conception is wrong,
but because it is, I am afraid, forgotten, and
also because we carry it to a degree not
reached in any other country. Griffis [1] was

[1] *Religions of Japan.*

quite right in stating that whereas in China Confucian ethics made obedience to parents the primary human duty, in Japan precedence was given to loyalty. At the risk of shocking some of my good readers, I will relate of one "who could endure to follow a fall'n lord" and who thus, as Shakespeare assures, "earned a place i' the story."

The story is of one of the greatest characters of our history, Michizané, who, falling a victim to jealousy and calumny, is exiled from the capital. Not content with this, his unrelenting enemies are now bent upon the extinction of his family. Strict search for his son—not yet grown—reveals the fact of his being secreted in a village school kept by one Genzo, a former vassal of Michizané. When orders are dispatched to the schoolmaster to deliver the head of the juvenile offender on a certain day, his first idea is to find a suitable substitute for it. He ponders over his school-list, scrutinises with careful eyes all the boys, as they stroll into the class-room, but none among the children born of the soil bears the least resemblance to his protégé. His despair, however, is but for a moment; for, behold, a new scholar is announced—a comely boy of the same age as his master's son, escorted by a mother of noble mien.

No less conscious of the resemblance between infant lord and infant retainer, were the mother and the boy himself. In the privacy of home both had laid themselves upon the altar; the one his life—the other her heart, yet without sign to the outer world. Unwitting of what had passed between them, it is the teacher from whom comes the suggestion.

Here, then, is the scapegoat!—The rest of the narrative may be briefly told.—On the day appointed, arrives the officer commissioned to identify and receive the head of the youth. Will he be deceived by the false head? The poor Genzo's hand is on the hilt of the sword, ready to strike a blow either at the man or at himself, should the examination defeat his scheme. The officer takes up the gruesome object before him, goes calmly over each feature, and in a deliberate, business-like tone, pronounces it genuine.—That evening in a lonely home awaits the mother we saw in the school. Does she know the fate of her child? It is not for his return that she watches with eagerness for the opening of the wicket. Her father-in-law has been for a long time a recipient of Michizané's bounties, but since his banishment, circumstances have forced her husband to follow the service of the enemy of his family's benefactor. He himself could not be untrue to his own cruel master; but his son could serve the cause of the grandsire's lord. As one acquainted with the exile's family, it was he who had been entrusted with the task of identifying the boy's head. Now the day's—yea, the life's— hard work is done, he returns home and as he crosses its threshold, he accosts his wife, saying: "Rejoice, my wife, our darling son has proved of service to his lord!"

"What an atrocious story!" I hear my readers exclaim. "Parents deliberately sacrificing their own innocent child to save the

life of another man's!" But this child was a
conscious and willing victim: it is a story of
vicarious death—as significant as, and not
more revolting than, the story of Abraham's
intended sacrifice of Isaac. In both cases was
obedience to the call of duty, utter submission
to the command of a higher voice, whether
given by a visible or an invisible angel, or
heard by an outward or an inward ear;—but
I abstain from preaching.

The individualism of the West, which
recognises separate interests for father and
son, husband and wife, necessarily brings into
strong relief the duties owed by one to the
other; but Bushido held that the interest of
the family and of the members thereof is
intact,—one and inseparable. This interest
it bound up with affection—natural, instinc-
tive, irresistible; hence, if we die for one we
love with natural love (which animals themselves possess), what is that? "For if ye
love them that love you, what reward have
ye? Do not even the publicans the same?"

In his great history, Sanyo relates in

touching language the heart struggle of Shigemori concerning his father's rebellious conduct. "If I be loyal, my father must be undone; if I obey my father, my duty to my sovereign must go amiss." Poor Shigemori! We see him afterward praying with all his soul that kind Heaven may visit him with death, that he may be released from this world where it is hard for purity and right-eousness to dwell.

Many a Shigemori has his heart torn by the conflict between duty and affection. Indeed, neither Shakespeare nor the Old Testament itself contains an adequate rendering of *ko*, our conception of filial piety, and yet in such conflicts Bushido never wavered in its choice of loyalty. Women, too, encouraged their offspring to sacrifice all for the king. Even as resolute as Widow Windham and her illus-trious consort, the samurai matron stood ready to give up her boys for the cause of loyalty.

Since Bushido, like Aristotle and some modern sociologists, conceived the state as antedating the individual,—the latter being born into the former as part and parcel thereof,—he must live and die for it or for the incumbent of its legitimate authority. Readers of Crito will remember the argument with which Socrates represents the laws of the city as pleading with him on the subject of his escape. Among others he makes them (the laws or the state) say: "Since you were begotten and nurtured and educated under us, dare you once to say you are not our offspring and servant, you and your fathers before you?" These are words which do not impress us as any thing extraordinary; for the same thing has long been on the lips of Bushido, with this modification, that the laws and the state were represented with us by a personal being. Loyalty is an ethical outcome of this political theory.

I am not entirely ignorant of Mr. Spencer's view according to which political obedience—loyalty—is accredited with only a transitional function.[1] It may be so. Sufficient

[1] *Principles of Ethics*, Vol. I., pt. ii., ch. x.

unto the day is the virtue thereof. We may complacently repeat it, especially as we believe *that* day to be a long space of time, during which, so our national anthem says, "tiny pebbles grow into mighty rocks draped with moss."

We may remember at this juncture that even among so democratic a people as the English, "the sentiment of personal fidelity to a man and his posterity which their Germanic ancestors felt for their chiefs, has," as Monsieur Boutmy recently said, "only passed more or less into their profound loyalty to the race and blood of their princes, as evidenced in their extraordinary attachment to the dynasty."

Political subordination, Mr. Spencer predicts, will give place to loyalty, to the dictates of conscience. Suppose his induction is realised—will loyalty and its concomitant instinct of reverence disappear forever? We transfer our allegiance from one master to another, without being unfaithful to either: from being subjects of a ruler that wields the temporal sceptre we become servants of the monarch who sits enthroned in the penetralia of our hearts. A few years ago a very stupid controversy, started by the misguided disciples of Spencer, made havoc among the reading class of Japan. In their zeal to uphold the claim of the throne to undivided loyalty, they charged Christians with treasonable propensity in that they avow fidelity to their Lord and Master. They arrayed forth sophistical arguments without the wit of Sophists, and scholastic tortuosities minus the niceties of the Schoolmen. Little did they know that we can, in a sense, "serve two masters without holding to the one or despising the other," "rendering unto Cæsar the things that are Cæsar's and unto God the things that are God's." Did not Socrates, all the while he unflinchingly refused to concede one iota of loyalty to his *dæmon*, obey with equal fidelity and equanimity the command of his earthly master, the State? His conscience he followed, alive; his country he served, dying. Alack the day when a state grows so powerful as to demand of its citizens the dictates of their conscience!

Bushido did not require us to make our conscience the slave of any lord or king. Thomas Mowbray was a veritable spokesman for us when he said:

"Myself I throw, dread sovereign, at thy foot.
  My life thou shall command, but not my shame.
  The one my duty owes; but my fair name,
  Despite of death, that lives upon my grave,
  To dark dishonour's use, thou shall not have."

A man who sacrificed his own conscience to the capricious will or freak or fancy of a sovereign was accorded a low place in the estimate of the Precepts. Such an one was despised as *nei-shin*, a cringeling, who makes court by unscrupulous fawning, or as *chô-shin*, a favourite who steals his master's affections by means of servile compliance; these two species of subjects corresponding exactly to those which Iago describes,—the one, a duteous and knee-crooking knave, doting on his own obsequious bondage, wearing out his time much like his master's ass; the other trimming in forms and visages of duty, keeping yet his heart attending on himself. When a subject differed from his master, the loyal path for him to pursue was to use every available means to persuade him of his error, as Kent did to King Lear. Failing in this, let the master deal with him as he wills. In cases of this kind, it was quite a usual course for the samurai to make the last appeal to the intelligence and conscience of his lord by demonstrating the sincerity of his words with the shedding of his own blood.

Life being regarded as the means whereby to serve his master, and its ideal being set upon honour, the whole education and training of a samurai were conducted accordingly.

CHAPTER X

THE first point to observe in knightly pedagogics was to build up character, leaving in the shade the subtler faculties of prudence, intelligence and dialectics. We have seen the important part æsthetic accomplishments played in his education. Indispensable as they were to a man of culture, they were accessories rather than essentials of samurai training. Intellectual superiority was, of course, esteemed; but the word *Chi*, which was employed to denote intellectuality, meant wisdom in the first instance and gave knowledge only a very subordinate place. The tripod which supported the framework of Bushido was said to be *Chi*, *Jin*, *Yu*, respectively, Wisdom, Benevolence, and Courage. A samurai was essentially a man of action. Science was

94

without the pale of his activity. He took advantage of it in so far as it concerned his profession of arms. Religion and theology were relegated to the priests; he concerned himself with them in so far as they helped to nourish courage. Like an English poet the samurai believed "'t is not the creed that saves the man; but it is the man that justifies the creed." Philosophy and literature formed the chief part of his intellectual training; but even in the pursuit of these, it was not objective truth that he strove after,—literature was pursued mainly as a pastime, and philosophy as a practical aid in the formation of character, if not for the exposition of some military or political problem.

From what has been said, it will not be surprising to note that the curriculum of studies, according to the pedagogics of Bushido, consisted mainly of the following: —fencing, archery, *jiujutsu* [1] or *yawara*,

[1] The same word as that misspelled jiu-jitsu in common English parlance. It is the gentle art. It "uses no weapon." (W. E. G.)

horsemanship, the use of the spear, tactics, caligraphy, ethics, literature, and history. Of these, *jiujutsu* and caligraphy may require a few words of explanation. Great stress was laid on good writing, probably because our logograms, partaking as they do of the nature of pictures, possess artistic value, and also because chirography was accepted as indicative of one's personal character. *Jiujutsu* may be briefly defined as an application of anatomical knowledge to the purpose of offence or defence. It differs from wrestling, in that it does not depend upon muscular strength. It differs from other forms of attack in that it uses no weapons. Its feat consists in clutching or striking such part of the enemy's body as will make him numb and incapable of resistance. Its object is not to kill, but to incapacitate one for action for the time being.

A subject of study which one would expect to find in military education and which is rather conspicuous by its absence in the Bushido course of instruction, is mathematics.

This, however, can be readily explained in part by the fact that feudal warfare was not carried on with scientific precision. Not only that, but the whole training of the samurai was unfavourable to fostering numerical notions.

Chivalry is uneconomical: it boasts of penury. It says with Ventidius that "ambition, the soldier's virtue, rather makes choice of loss, than gain which darkens him." Don Quixote takes more pride in his rusty spear and skin-and-bone horse than in gold and lands, and a samurai is in hearty sympathy with his exaggerated confrère of La Mancha. He disdains money itself,—the art of making or hoarding it. It was to him veritably filthy lucre. The hackneyed expression to describe the decadence of an age was "that the civilians loved money and the soldiers feared death." Niggardliness of gold and of life excited as much disapprobation as their lavish use was panegyrised. "Less than all things," says a current precept, ' men must grudge money: it is by riches that wisdom is hindered." Hence children were brought up with utter disregard of economy. It was considered bad taste to speak of it, and ignorance of the value of different coins was a token of good breeding. Knowledge of numbers was indispensable in the mustering of forces as well as in distribution of benefices and fiefs; but the counting of money was left to meaner hands. In many feudatories, public finance was administered by a lower kind of samurai or by priests. Every thinking bushi knew well enough that money formed the sinews of war; but he did not think of raising the appreciation of money to a virtue. It is true that thrift was enjoined by Bushido, but not for economical reasons so much as for the exercise of abstinence. Luxury was thought the greatest menace to manhood and severest simplicity of living was required of the warrior class, sumptuary laws being enforced in many of the clans.

We read that in ancient Rome the farmers of revenue and other financial agents were gradually raised to the rank of knights, the

State thereby showing its appreciation of their service and of the importance of money itself. How closely this is connected with the luxury and avarice of the Romans may be imagined. Not so with the Precepts of Knighthood. It persisted in systematically regarding finance as something low—low as compared with moral and intellectual vocations.

Money and the love of it being thus diligently ignored, Bushido itself could long remain free from a thousand and one evils of which money is the root. This is sufficient reason for the fact that our public men have long been free from corruption; but alas! how fast plutocracy is making its way in our time and generation.

The mental discipline which would nowadays be chiefly aided by the study of mathematics, was supplied by literary exegesis and deontological discussions. Very few abstract subjects troubled the mind of the young, the chief aim of their education being, as I have said, decision of character. People whose minds were simply stored with information found no great admirers. Of the three services of studies that Bacon gives,—for delight, ornament, and ability,—Bushido had decided preference for the last, where their use was "in judgment and the disposition of business." Whether it was for the disposition of public business or for the exercise of self-control, it was with a practical end in view that education was conducted. "Learning without thought," said Confucius, "is labour lost; thought without learning is perilous."

When character and not intelligence, when the soul and not the head, is chosen by a teacher for the material to work upon and to develop, his vocation partakes of a sacred character. "It is the parent who has borne me: it is the teacher who makes me man." With this idea, therefore, the esteem in which one's preceptor was held was very high. A man to evoke such confidence and respect from the young, must necessarily be endowed with superior personality, without lacking

erudition.   He was a father to the fatherless,
and an adviser to the erring.   "Thy father
and thy mother."—so runs our maxim—"are
like heaven and earth; thy teacher and thy
lord are like the sun and moon."

The present system of paying for every sort
of service was not in vogue among the ad-
herents of Bushido.   It believed in a service
which can be rendered only without money
and without price.   Spiritual service, be it of
priest or teacher, was not to be repaid in gold
or silver, not because it was valueless but because it was invaluable.   Here the non-arith-
metical honour - instinct of Bushido taught a
truer lesson than modern Political Economy;
for wages and salaries can be paid only for
services whose results are definite, tangible,
and measurable, whereas the best service
done in education,—namely, in soul development (and this includes the services of a pas-
tor), is not definite, tangible, or measurable.
Being immeasurable, money, the ostensible
measure of value, is of inadequate use.
Usage sanctioned that pupils brought to their

teachers money or goods at different seasons
of the year; but these were not payments but
offerings, which indeed were welcome to the
recipients as they were usually men of stern
calibre, boasting of honourable penury, too
dignified to work with their hands and too
proud to beg. They were grave personifica-
tions of high spirits undaunted by adversity.
They were an embodiment of what was considered as an end of all learning, and were
thus a living example of that discipline of
disciplines, self-control, which was universally
required of samurai.

CHAPTER XI

SELF-CONTROL

THE discipline of fortitude on the one hand, inculcating endurance without a groan, and the teaching of politeness on the other, requiring us not to mar the pleasure or serenity of another by expressions of our own sorrow or pain, combined to engender a stocial turn of mind, and eventually to confirm it into a national trait of apparent stoicism. I say apparent stoicism, because I do not believe that true stoicism can ever become the characteristic of a whole nation, and also because some of our national manners and customs may seem to a foreign observer hard-hearted. Yet we are really as susceptible to tender emotion as any race under the sky.

I am inclined to think that in one sense we

have to feel more than others—yes, doubly more—since the very attempt to restrain natural promptings entails suffering. Imagine boys—and girls, too—brought up not to resort to the shedding of a tear or the uttering of a groan for the relief of their feelings,—and there is a physiological problem whether such effort steels their nerves or makes them more sensitive.

It was considered unmanly for a samurai to betray his emotions on his face. "He shows no sign of joy or anger," was a phrase used, in describing a great character. The most natural affections were kept under control. A father could embrace his son only at the expense of his dignity; a husband would not kiss his wife,—no, not in the presence of other people, whatever he might do in private! There may be some truth in the remark of a witty youth when he said, "American husbands kiss their wives in public and beat them in private; Japanese husbands beat theirs in public and kiss them in private."

Calmness of behaviour, composure of mind,

should not be disturbed by passion of any kind. I remember when, during the late war with China, a regiment left a certain town, a large concourse of people flocked to the station to bid farewell to the general and his army. On this occasion an American resident resorted to the place, expecting to witness loud demonstrations, as the nation itself was highly excited and there were fathers, mothers, wives, and sweethearts of the soldiers in the crowd. The American was strangely disappointed; for as the whistle blew and the train began to move, the hats of thousands of people were silently taken off and their heads bowed in reverential farewell; no waving of handkerchiefs, no word uttered, but deep silence in which only an attentive ear could catch a few broken sobs. In domestic life, too, I know of a father who spent whole nights listening to the breathing of a sick child, standing behind the door that he might not be caught in such an act of parental weakness! I know of a mother who, in her last moments, refrained from sending for her

son, that he might not be disturbed in his
studies.   Our history and everyday life are
replete with examples of heroic matrons who
can well bear comparison with some of the
most touching pages of Plutarch.   Among
our peasantry an Ian Maclaren would be sure
to find many a Marget Howe.

It is the same discipline of self-restraint
which is accountable for the absence of more
frequent revivals in the Christian churches of
Japan.   When a man or woman feels his or
her soul stirred, the first instinct is quietly to
suppress the manifestation of it.   In rare
instances is the tongue set free by an irresistible spirit, when we have eloquence of sincerity
and fervour.   It is putting a premium upon a
breach of the third commandment to encourage speaking lightly of spiritual experience.   It is truly jarring to Japanese ears to
hear the most sacred words, the most secret
heart experiences, thrown out in promiscuous
audiences.   "Dost thou feel the soil of thy
soul stirred with tender thoughts?   It is time
for seeds to sprout.   Disturb it not with

speech; but let it work alone in quietness and secrecy,"—writes a young samurai in his diary.

To give in so many articulate words one's inmost thoughts and feelings—notably the religious—is taken among us as an unmistakable sign that they are neither very profound nor very sincere. "Only a pomegranate is he"—so runs a popular saying "who, when he gapes his mouth, displays the contents of his heart."

It is not altogether perverseness of oriental minds that the instant our emotions are moved, we try to guard our lips in order to hide them. Speech is very often with us, as the Frenchman defines it, "the art of concealing thought."

Call upon a Japanese friend in time of deepest affliction and he will invariably receive you laughing, with red eyes or moist cheeks. At first you may think him hysterical. Press him for explanation and you will get a few broken commonplaces—" Human life has sorrow"; "They who meet must part"; "He that is born must die"; "It is foolish to count the years of a child that is gone, but a woman's heart will indulge in follies"; and the like. So the noble words of a noble Hohenzollern—"Lerne zu leiden ohne klagen"—had found many responsive minds among us long before they were uttered.

Indeed, the Japanese have recourse to risibility whenever the frailties of human nature are put to severest test. I think we possess a better reason than Democritus himself for our Abderian tendency, for laughter with us oftenest veils an effort to regain balance of temper when disturbed by any untoward circumstance. It is a counterpoise of sorrow or rage.

The suppression of feelings being thus steadily insisted upon, they find their safety-valve in poetical aphorisms. A poet of the tenth century writes "In Japan and China as well, humanity, when moved by sorrow, tells its bitter grief in verse." A mother who tries to console her broken heart by fancying her departed child absent on his wonted chase after the dragon-fly hums,

> " How far to-day in chase, I wonder,
> Has gone my hunter of the dragon-fly! "

I refrain from quoting other examples, for I know I could do only scant justice to the pearly gems of our literature, were I to render into a foreign tongue the thoughts which were wrung drop by drop from bleeding hearts and threaded into beads of rarest value. I hope I have in a measure shown that inner working of our minds which often presents an appearance of callousness or of an hysterical mixture of laughter and dejection, and whose sanity is sometimes called in question.

It has also been suggested that our endurance of pain and indifference to death are due to less sensitive nerves. This is plausible as far as it goes. The next question is,—Why are our nerves less tightly strung? It may be our climate is not so stimulating as the American. It may be our monarchical form of government does not excite us so much as the Republic does the Frenchman. It may be that we do not read *Sartor Resartus* so zealously as the Englishman. Personally, I believe it was our very excitability and sensitiveness which made it a necessity to recognise and enforce constant self-repression; but whatever may be the explanation, without taking into account long years of discipline in self-control, none can be correct.

Discipline in self-control can easily go too far. It can well repress the genial current of the soul. It can force pliant natures into distortions and monstrosities. It can beget bigotry, breed hypocrisy, or hebetate affections. Be a virtue never so noble, it has its counterpart and counterfeit. We must recognise in each virtue its own positive excellence and follow its positive ideal, and the ideal of self-restraint is to keep the mind level—as our expression is—or, to borrow a Greek term, attain the state of *euthymia*, which Democritus called the highest good.

The acme and pitch of self-control is reached and best illustrated in the first of the two institutions which we shall now bring to view, namely, the institutions of suicide and redress.

CHAPTER XII

THE INSTITUTIONS OF SUICIDE AND REDRESS

OF these two institutions (the former known as *hara-kiri* and the latter as *kataki-uchi*), many foreign writers have treated more or less fully.

To begin with suicide, let me state that I confine my observations only to *seppuku* or *kappuku*, popularly known as *hara-kiri*—which means self-immolation by disembowelment. "Ripping the abdomen? How absurd!"—so cry those to whom the name is new. Absurdly odd as it may sound at first to foreign ears, it cannot be so very foreign to students of Shakespeare, who puts these words in Brutus's mouth—"Thy [Cæsar's] spirit walks abroad and turns our swords into our proper entrails." Listen to a modern

English poet who, in his *Light of Asia*, speaks of a sword piercing the bowels of a queen;— none blames him for bad English or breach of modesty. Or, to take still another example, look at Guercino's painting of Cato's death in the Palazzo Rossa, in Genoa. Whoever has read the swan-song which Addison makes Cato sing, will not jeer at the sword half-buried in his abdomen. In our minds this mode of death is associated with instances of noblest deeds and of most touching pathos, so that nothing repugnant, much less ludicrous, mars our conception of it. So wonderful is the transforming power of virtue, of greatness, of tenderness, that the vilest form of death assumes a sublimity and becomes a symbol of new life, or else—the sign which Constantine beheld would not conquer the world!

Not for extraneous associations only does *seppuku* lose in our mind any taint of absurdity; for the choice of this particular part of the body to operate upon, was based on an old anatomical belief as to the seat of the soul and of the affections. When Moses

wrote of Joseph's "bowels yearning upon
his brother," or David prayed the Lord not
to forget his bowels, or when Isaiah, Jeremiah, and other inspired men of old spoke of
the "sounding" or the "troubling" of bowels,
they all and each endorsed the belief prevalent
among the Japanese that in the abdomen was
enshrined the soul. The Semites habitually
spoke of the liver and kidneys and surround-
ing fat as the seat of emotion and of life. The
term *"hara"* was more comprehensive than
the Greek *phren* or *thumos*, and the Japanese
and Hellenese alike thought the spirit of man
to dwell somewhere in that region. Such a
notion is by no means confined to the peoples
of antiquity. The French, in spite of the
theory propounded by one of their most
distinguished philosophers, Descartes, that
the soul is located in the pineal gland, still
insist in using the term *ventre* in a sense
which, if anatomically too vague, is nevertheless physiologically significant. Similarly, *en-
trailles* stands in their language for affection
and compassion. Nor is such a belief mere

superstition, being more scientific than the general idea of making the heart the centre of the feelings. Without asking a friar, the Japanese knew better than Romeo "in what vile part of this anatomy one's name did lodge." Modern neurologists speak of the abdominal and pelvic brains, denoting thereby sympathetic nerve centres in those parts which are strongly affected by any psychical action. This view of mental physiology once admitted, the syllogism of *seppuku* is easy to construct. "I will open the seat of my soul and show you how it fares with it. See for yourself whether it is polluted or clean."

I do not wish to be understood as asserting religious or even moral justification of suicide, but the high estimate placed upon honour was ample excuse with many for taking one's own life. How many acquiesced in the sentiment expressed by Garth,

> "When honour's lost, 't is a relief to die;
> Death's but a sure retreat from infamy,"

and have smilingly surrendered their souls to

oblivion! Death involving a question of honour, was accepted in Bushido as a key to the solution of many complex problems, so that to an ambitious samurai a natural departure from life seemed a rather tame affair and a consummation not devoutly to be wished for. I dare say that many good Christians, if only they are honest enough, will confess the fascination of, if not positive admiration for, the sublime composure with which Cato, Brutus, Petronius, and a host of other ancient worthies terminated their own earthly existence. Is it too bold to hint that the death of the first of the philosophers was partly suicidal? When we are told so minutely by his pupils how their master willingly submitted to the mandate of the state—which he knew was morally mistaken—in spite of the possibilities of escape, and how he took the cup of hemlock in his own hand, even offering libation from its deadly contents, do we not discern, in his whole proceeding and demeanour, an act of self-immolation? No physical compulsion here, as in ordinary cases of execution. True, the verdict of the judges was compulsory: it said, "Thou shalt die,—and that by thine own hand." If suicide meant no more than dying by one's own hand, Socrates was a clear case of suicide. But nobody would charge him with the crime; Plato, who was averse to it, would not call his master a suicide.

Now my readers will understand that *seppuku* was not a mere suicidal process. It was an institution, legal and ceremonial. An invention of the middle ages, it was a process by which warriors could expiate their crimes, apologise for errors, escape from disgrace, redeem their friends, or prove their sincerity. When enforced as a legal punishment, it was practised with due ceremony. It was a refinement of self-destruction, and none could perform it without the utmost coolness of temper and composure of demeanour, and for these reasons it was particularly befitting the profession of bushi.

Antiquarian curiosity, if nothing else, would tempt me to give here a description of this obsolete ceremony; but seeing that such a description was made by a far abler writer, whose book is not much read nowadays, I am tempted to make a somewhat lengthy quotation. Mitford, in his *Tales of Old Japan*, after giving a translation of a treatise on *seppuku* from a rare Japanese manuscript, goes on to describe an instance of such an execution of which he was an eye-witness:

"We (seven foreign representatives) were invited to follow the Japanese witnesses into the *hondo* or main hall of the temple, where the ceremony was to be performed. It was an imposing scene. A large hall with a high roof supported by dark pillars of wood. From the ceiling hung a profusion of those huge gilt lamps and ornaments peculiar to Buddhist temples. In front of the high altar, where the floor, covered with beautiful white mats, is raised some three or four inches from the ground, was laid a rug of scarlet felt. Tall candles placed at regular intervals gave out a dim mysterious light, just sufficient to let all the proceedings be seen. The seven Japanese took their places on the left of the raised floor, the seven foreigners on the right. No other person was present.

" After the interval of a few minutes of anxious suspense, Taki Zenzaburo, a stalwart man thirty-two years of age, with a noble air, walked into the hall attired in his dress of ceremony, with the peculiar hempen-cloth wings which are worn on great occasions. He was accompanied by a *kaishaku* and three officers, who wore the *jimbaori* or war surcoat with gold tissue facings. The word *kaishaku*, it should be observed, is one to which our word executioner is no equivalent term. The office is that of a gentleman; in many cases it is performed by a kinsman or friend of the condemned, and the relation between them is rather that of principal and second than that of victim and executioner. In this instance, the *kaishaku* was a pupil of Taki Zenzaburo, and was selected by friends of the latter from among their own number for his skill in swordsmanship.

"With the *kaishaku* on his left hand, Taki Zenzaburo advanced slowly toward the Japanese witnesses, and the two bowed before them, then drawing near to the foreigners they saluted us in the same way, perhaps even with more deference; in each case the salutation was ceremoniously returned. Slowly and with great dignity the condemned man mounted on to the raised floor, prostrated himself before the high altar twice, and seated [1] himself on the felt carpet with his back to the high altar, the *kaishaku* crouching on his left-hand side. One of the three attendant officers then came forward, bearing a stand of the kind used in the temple for offerings, on which,

---

[1] Seated himself—that is, in the Japanese fashion, his knees and toes touching the ground and his body resting on his heels. In this position, which is one of respect, he remained until his death.

wrapped in paper, lay the *wakizashi*, the short sword or dirk of the Japanese, nine inches and a half in length, with a point and an edge as sharp as a razor's. This he handed, prostrating himself, to the condemned man, who received it reverently raising it to his head with both hands, and placed it in front of himself.

"After another profound obeisance, Taki Zenzaburo, in a voice which betrayed just so much emotion and hesitation as might be expected from a man who is making a painful confession, but with no sign of either in his face or manner, spoke as follows:—

"'I, and I alone, unwarrantably gave the order to fire on the foreigners at Kobe, and again as they tried to escape. For this crime I disembowel myself, and I beg you who are present to do me the honour of witnessing the act.'

"Bowing once more, the speaker allowed his upper garments to slip down to his girdle, and remained naked to the waist. Carefully, according to custom, he tucked his sleeves under his knees to prevent himself from falling backward; for a noble Japanese gentleman should die falling forwards Deliberately, with a steady hand he took the dirk that lay before him; he looked at it wistfully, almost affectionately; for a moment he seemed to collect his thoughts for the last time, and then stabbing himself deeply below the waist in the left-hand side, he drew the dirk slowly across to his right side, and turning it in the wound, gave a slight cut upwards. During this sickeningly painful operation he never moved a muscle of his face.

When he drew out the dirk, he leaned forward and stretched out his neck; an expression of pain for the first time crossed his face, but he uttered no sound. At that moment the *kaishaku*, who, still crouching by his side, had been keenly watching his every movement, sprang to his feet, poised his sword for a second in the air; there was a flash, a heavy, ugly thud, a crashing fall; with one blow the head had been severed from the body.

"A dead silence followed, broken only by the hideous noise of the blood throbbing out of the inert heap before us, which but a moment before had been a brave and chivalrous man. It was horrible.

"The *kaishaku* made a low bow, wiped his sword with a piece of paper which he had ready for the purpose, and retired from the raised floor; and the stained dirk was solemnly borne away, a bloody proof of the execution.

"The two representatives of the Mikado then left their places, and crossing over to where the foreign witnesses sat, called to us to witness that the sentence of death upon Taki Zenzaburo had been faithfully carried out. The ceremony being at an end, we left the temple."

I might multiply any number of descriptions of *seppuku* from literature or from the relations of eye-witnesses; but one more instance will suffice.

Two brothers, Sakon and Naiki, respec-

tively twenty-four and seventeen years of age,
made an effort to kill Iyéyasu in order to
avenge their father's wrongs; but before
they could enter the camp they were made
prisoners. The old general admired the pluck
of the youths who dared an attempt on his
life and ordered that they should be allowed
to die an honourable death. Their little
brother Hachimaro, a mere infant of eight
summers, was condemned to a similar fate,
as the sentence was pronounced on all the
male members of the family, and the three
were taken to a monastery where it was to be
executed. A physician who was present on
the occasion has left us a diary, from which
the following scene is translated:

"When they were all seated in a row for final
despatch, Sakon turned to the youngest and said—
'Go thou first, for I wish to be sure that thou doest
it aright.' Upon the little one's replying that, as
he had never seen *seppuku* performed, he would
like to see his brothers do it and then he could
follow them, the older brothers smiled between
their tears:—'Well said, little fellow! So canst
thou well boast of being our father's child.' When
they had placed him between them, Sakon thrust

the dagger into the left side of his abdomen and said—'Look brother! Dost understand now? Only, don't push the dagger too far, lest thou fall back. Lean forward, rather, and keep thy knees well composed.' Naiki did likewise and said to the boy—'Keep thine eyes open or else thou mayst look like a dying woman. If thy dagger feels anything within and thy strength fails, take courage and double thy effort to cut across.' The child looked from one to the other, and, when both had expired, he calmly half denuded himself and followed the example set him on either hand."

The glorification of *seppuku* offered, naturally enough, no small temptation to its unwarranted committal. For causes entirely incompatible with reason, or for reasons entirely undeserving of death, hot-headed youths rushed into it as insects fly into fire; mixed and dubious motives drove more samurai to this deed than nuns into convent gates. Life was cheap—cheap as reckoned by the popular standard of honour. The saddest feature was that honour, which was always in the *agio*, so to speak, was not always solid gold, but alloyed with baser metals. No one circle in the Inferno will boast of greater density of Japanese population than the seventh, to which Dante consigns all victims of self-destruction!

And yet, for a true samurai to hasten death or to court it, was alike cowardice. A typical fighter, when he lost battle after battle and was pursued from plain to hill and from bush to cavern, found himself hungry and alone in the dark hollow of a tree, his sword blunt with use, his bow broken and arrows exhausted—did not the noblest of the Romans fall upon his own sword in Philippi under like circumstances?—deemed it cowardly to die, but, with a fortitude approaching a Christian martyr's, cheered himself with an impromptu verse:

> "Come! evermore come,
>   Ye dread sorrows and pains!
> And heap on my burden'd back;
> That I not one test may lack
>   Of what strength in me remains!"

This, then, was the Bushido teaching—Bear and face all calamities and adversities with patience and a pure conscience; for, as Mencius [1] taught, "When Heaven is about to

[1] I use Dr. Legge's translation verbatim.

confer a great office on anyone, it first exercises his mind with suffering and his sinews and bones with toil; it exposes his body to hunger and subjects him to extreme poverty; and it confounds his undertakings. In all these ways it stimulates his mind, hardens his nature, and supplies his incompetencies." True honour lies in fulfilling Heaven's decree and no death incurred in so doing is ignominious, whereas, death to avoid what Heaven has in store is cowardly indeed! In that quaint book of Sir Thomas Browne's, *Religio Medici*, there is an exact English equivalent for what is repeatedly taught in our Precepts. Let me quote it: "It is a brave act of valour to contemn death, but where life is more terrible than death, it is then the truest valour to dare to live." A renowned priest of the seventeenth century satirically observed —"Talk as he may, a samurai who ne'er has died is apt in decisive moments to flee or hide." Again—"Him who once has died in the bottom of his breast, no spears of Sanada nor all the arrows of Tametomo can pierce."

How near we come to the portals of the temple whose Builder taught "He that loseth his life for my sake shall find it"! These are but a few of the numerous examples that tend to confirm the moral identity of the human species, notwithstanding an attempt so assiduously made to render the distinction between Christian and Pagan as great as possible.

We have thus seen that the Bushido institution of suicide was neither so irrational nor barbarous as its abuse strikes us at first sight. We will now see whether its sister institution of Redress—or call it Revenge, if you will—has its mitigating features. I hope I can dispose of this question in a few words, since a similar institution, or call it custom, if that suits you better, prevailed among all peoples and has not yet become entirely obsolete, as attested by the continuance of duelling and lynching. Why, has not an American captain recently challenged Esterhazy, that the wrongs of Dreyfus be avenged? Among a savage tribe which has

no marriage, adultery is not a sin, and only
the jealousy of a lover protects a woman from
abuse; so in a time which has no criminal
court, murder is not a crime, and only the
vigilant vengeance of the victim's people pre-
serves social order. "What is the most
beautiful thing on earth?" said Osiris to
Horus. The reply was, "To avenge a parent's
wrongs,"—to which a Japanese would have
added "and a master's."

In revenge there is something which satis-
fies one's sense of justice. The avenger
reasons:—"My good father did not deserve
death. He who killed him did great evil.
My father, if he were alive, would not tolerate
a deed like this: Heaven itself hates wrong-
doing. It is the will of my father; it is the
will of Heaven that the evil-doer cease from
his work. He must perish by my hand; because he shed my father's blood, I, who am his
flesh and blood, must shed the murderer's.
The same Heaven shall not shelter him and
me." The ratiocination is simple and child-
ish (though we know Hamlet did not reason

much more deeply); nevertheless it shows an innate sense of exact balance and equal justice. "An eye for an eye, a tooth for a tooth." Our sense of revenge is as exact as our mathematical faculty, and until both terms of the equation are satisfied we cannot get over the sense of something left undone.

In Judaism, which believed in a jealous God, or in Greek mythology, which provided a Nemesis, vengeance may be left to super-human agencies; but common sense furnished Bushido with the institution of redress as a kind of ethical court of equity, where people could take cases not to be judged in accord-ance with ordinary law. The master of the forty-seven Ronins was condemned to death; he had no court of higher instance to appeal to; his faithful retainers addressed them-selves to vengeance, the only Supreme Court existing; they in their turn were condemned by common law,—but the popular instinct passed a different judgment, and hence their memory is still kept as green and fragrant as are their graves at Sengakuji to this day.

Though Lâo-tse taught to recompense injury with kindness, the voice of Confucius was very much louder, which taught that injury must be recompensed with justice;—and yet revenge was justified only when it was undertaken in behalf of our superiors and benefactors. One's own wrongs, including injuries done to wife and children, were to be borne and forgiven. A samurai could therefore fully sympathise with Hannibal's oath to avenge his country's wrongs, but he scorns James Hamilton for wearing in his girdle a handful of earth from his wife's grave, as an eternal incentive to avenge her wrongs on the Regent Murray.

Both of these institutions of suicide and redress lost their *raison d'être* at the promulgation of the Criminal Code. No more do we hear of romantic adventures of a fair maiden as she tracks in disguise the murderer of her parent. No more can we witness tragedies of family vendetta enacted. The knight errantry of Miyamoto Musashi is now a tale of the past. The well-ordered police spies out the criminal for the injured party and the law metes out justice. The whole state and society will see that wrong is righted. The sense of justice satisfied, there is no need of *kataki-uchi*. If this had meant that "hunger of the heart which feeds upon the hope of glutting that hunger with the life blood of the victim," as a New England divine has described it, a few paragraphs in the Criminal Code would not so entirely have made an end of it.

As to *seppuku*, though it too has no existence *de jure*, we still hear of it from time to time, and shall continue to hear, I am afraid, as long as the past is remembered. Many painless and time-saving methods of self-immolation will come in vogue, as its votaries are increasing with fearful rapidity throughout the world; but Professor Morselli will have to concede to *seppuku* an aristocratic position among them. He maintains that "when suicide is accomplished by very painful means or at the cost of prolonged agony, in ninety-nine cases out of a hundred, it may be

assigned as the act of a mind disordered by
fanaticism, by madness, or by morbid excite-
ment." [1] But a normal *seppuku* does not
savour of fanaticism, or madness or excite-
ment, utmost *sang froid* being necessary to its
successful accomplishment. Of the two kinds
into which Dr. Strahan [2] divides suicide, the
Rational or Quasi, and the Irrational or True,
seppuku is the best example of the former
type.

From these bloody institutions, as well as
from the general tenor of Bushido, it is easy to
infer that the sword played an important part
in social discipline and life. The saying
passed as an axiom which called the sword
the soul of the samurai.

[1] Morselli, *Suicide*, p. 314
[2] *Suicide and Insanity*.

CHAPTER XIII

THE SWORD, THE SOUL OF THE SAMURAI

BUSHIDO made the sword its emblem of power and prowess. When Mahomet proclaimed that "the sword is the key of Heaven and of Hell," he only echoed a Japanese sentiment. Very early the samurai boy learned to wield it. It was a momentous occasion for him when at the age of five he was apparelled in the paraphernalia of samurai costume, placed upon a *go*-board [1] and initiated into the rights of the military profession, by having thrust into his girdle a real sword instead of the toy dirk with which he had been playing. After this first ceremony

[1] The game of *go* is sometimes called Japanese checkers, but is much more intricate than the English game. The *go*-board contains 361 squares and is supposed to represent a battle-field—the object of the game being to occupy as much space as possible.

of *adoptio per arma*, he was no more to be
seen outside his father's gates without this
badge of his status, even though it was usually substituted for everyday wear by a gilded
wooden dirk.   Not many years pass before he
wears constantly the genuine steel, though
blunt, and then the sham arms are thrown
aside and with enjoyment keener than his
newly acquired blades, he marches out to try
their edge on wood and stone.   When he
reaches man's estate, at the age of fifteen,
being given independence of action, he can
now pride himself upon the possession of
arms sharp enough for any work.   The very
possession of the dangerous instrument im-
parts to him a feeling and an air of self-
respect and responsibility.   "He beareth
not the sword in vain."   What he carries in
his belt is a symbol of what he carries in his
mind and heart,—loyalty and honour.   The
two swords, the longer and the shorter,—
called respectively *daito* and *shoto* or *katana*
and *wakizashi*,—never leave his side.   When
at home, they grace the most conspicuous

place in the study or parlour; by night they guard his pillow within easy reach of his hand. Constant companions, they are beloved, and proper names of endearment given them. Being venerated, they are well-nigh worshipped. The Father of History has recorded as a curious piece of information that the Scythians sacrificed to an iron scimitar. Many a temple and many a family in Japan hoards a sword as an object of adoration. Even the commonest dirk has due respect paid to it. Any insult to it is tantamount to personal affront. Woe to him who carelessly steps over a weapon lying on the floor!

So precious an object cannot long escape the notice and the skill of artists nor the vanity of its owner, especially in times of peace, when it is worn with no more use than a crosier by a bishop or a sceptre by a king. Sharkskin and finest silk for hilt, silver and gold for guard, lacquer of varied hues for scabbard, robbed the deadliest weapon of half its terror; but these appurtenances are playthings compared with the blade itself.

The swordsmith was not a mere artisan but an inspired artist and his workshop a sanctuary. Daily he commenced his craft with prayer and purification, or, as the phrase was, "he committed his soul and spirit into the forging and tempering of the steel." Every swing of the sledge, every plunge into water, every friction on the grindstone, was a religious act of no slight import. Was it the spirit of the master or of his tutelary god that cast a formidable spell over our sword? Perfect as a work of art, setting at defiance its Toledo and Damascus rivals, there was more than art could impart. Its cold blade, collecting on its surface the moment it is drawn the vapour of the atmosphere; its immaculate texture, flashing light of bluish hue; its matchless edge, upon which histories and possibilities hang; the curve of its back, uniting exquisite grace with utmost strength;—all these thrill us with mixed feelings of power and beauty, of awe and terror. Harmless were its mission, if it only remained a thing of beauty and joy! But, ever within reach of the hand, it presented no small temptation for abuse. Too often did the blade flash forth from its peaceful sheath. The abuse sometimes went so far as to try the acquired steel on some harmless creature's neck.

The question that concerns us most is, however,—Did Bushido justify the promiscuous use of the weapon? The answer is unequivocally, no! As it laid great stress on its proper use, so did it denounce and abhor its misuse. A dastard or a braggart was he who brandished his weapon on undeserved occasions. A self-possessed man knows the right time to use it, and such times come but rarely. Let us listen to the late Count Katsu, who passed through one of the most turbulent times of our history, when assassinations, suicides, and other sanguinary practices were the order of the day. Endowed as he once was with almost dictatorial powers, chosen repeatedly as an object of assassination, he never tarnished his sword with blood. In relating some of his reminiscences to a friend he says, in a quaint, plebeian way peculiar to him: "I have a great dislike for killing people and so I have n't killed one single man. I have released those whose heads should have been chopped off. A friend said to me one day, 'You don't kill enough. Don't you eat pepper and egg-plants?' Well, some people are no better! But you see that fellow was slain himself. My escape may be due to my dislike of killing. I had the hilt of my sword so tightly fastened to the scabbard that it was hard to draw the blade. I made up my mind that though they cut me, I would not cut. Yes, yes! some people are truly like fleas and mosquitoes and they bite—but what does their biting amount to? It itches a little, that's all; it won't endanger life." These are the words of one whose Bushido training was tried in the fiery furnace of adversity and triumph. The popular apothegm—"To be beaten is to conquer," meaning true conquest consists in not opposing a riotous foe; and "The best won victory is that obtained without shedding of blood," and others of similar import—will show that after all the ultimate ideal of knighthood was peace.

It was a great pity that this high ideal was left exclusively to priests and moralists to preach, while the samurai went on practising and extolling martial traits. In this they went so far as to tinge the ideals of womanhood with Amazonian character. Here we may profitably devote a few paragraphs to the subject of the training and position of woman.

CHAPTER XIV

THE TRAINING AND POSITION OF WOMAN

THE female half of our species has sometimes been called the paragon of paradoxes, because the intuitive working of its mind is beyond the comprehension of men's "arithemetical understanding." The Chinese ideogram denoting "the mysterious," "the unknowable," consists of two parts, one meaning "young" and the other "woman," because the physical charms and delicate thoughts of the fair sex are above the coarse mental calibre of our sex to explain.

In the Bushido ideal of woman, however, there is little mystery and only a seeming paradox. I have said that it was Amazonian, but that is only half the truth. Ideographically the Chinese represent wife by a woman

holding a broom—certainly not to brandish
it offensively or defensively against her con-
jugal ally, neither for witchcraft, but for the
more harmless uses for which the besom
was first invented—the idea involved being
thus not less homely than the etymological
derivation of the English wife (weaver) and
daughter (*duhitar*, milkmaid). Without con-
fining the sphere of woman's activity to
Küche, *Kirche*, *Kinder*, as the present German Kaiser is said to do, the Bushido ideal
of womanhood was pre-eminently domestic.
These seeming contradictions—domesticity
and Amazonian traits—are not inconsistent
with the Precepts of Knighthood, as we shall
see.

Bushido being a teaching primarily intended for the masculine sex, the virtues it
prized in woman were naturally far from
being distinctly feminine. Winckelmann remarks that "the supreme beauty of Greek art
is rather male than female," and Lecky adds
that it was true in the moral conception of
the Greeks as in their art. Bushido similarly

praised those women most "who emancipated themselves from the frailty of their sex and displayed an heroic fortitude worthy of the strongest and the bravest of men." [1] Young girls, therefore, were trained to repress their feelings, to indurate their nerves, to manipulate weapons,—especially the long-handled sword called *nagi-nata*, so as to be able to hold their own against unexpected odds. Yet the primary motive for exercise of this martial character was not for use in the field; it was twofold—personal and domestic. Woman owning no suzerain of her own, formed her own body-guard. With her weapon she guarded her personal sanctity with as much zeal as her husband did his master's. The domestic utility of her warlike training was in the education of her sons, as we shall see later.

Fencing and similar exercises, if rarely of practical use, were a wholesome counterbalance to the otherwise sedentary habits of women. But these exercises were not fol-

[1] Lecky, *History of European Morals*, ii., p. 383.

lowed only for hygienic purposes. They
could be turned into use in times of need.
Girls, when they reached womanhood, were
presented with dirks (*kai-ken*, pocket pon-
iards), which might be directed to the bosom
of their assailants, or, if advisable, to their
own. The latter was very often the case;
and yet I will not judge them severely. Even
the Christian conscience with its horror of
self-immolation, will not be harsh with them,
seeing Pelagia and Dominina, two suicides,
were canonised for their purity and piety.
When a Japanese Virginia saw her chastity
menaced, she did not wait for her father's
dagger. Her own weapon lay always in her
bosom. It was a disgrace to her not to know
the proper way in which she had to perpetrate
self-destruction. For example, little as she
was taught in anatomy, she must know the
exact spot to cut in her throat; she must
know how to tie her lower limbs together
with a belt so that, whatever the agonies of
death might be, her corpse be found in utmost
modesty with the limbs properly composed.

Is not a caution like this worthy of the
Christian Perpetua or the Vestal Cornelia? I
would not put such an abrupt interrogation
were it not for a misconception, based on our
bathing customs and other trifles, that chastity is unknown among us.[1] On the contrary, chastity was a pre-eminent virtue of
the samurai woman, held above life itself.
A young woman, taken prisoner, seeing herself in danger of violence at the hands of the
rough soldiery, says she will obey their pleasure, provided she be first allowed to write a
line to her sisters, whom war has dispersed in
every direction. When the epistle is finished,
off she runs to the nearest well and saves her
honour by drowning. The letter she leaves
behind ends with these verses:

> "For fear lest clouds may dim her light,
>   Should she but graze this nether sphere,
>   The young moon poised above the height
>   Doth hastily betake to flight."

It would be unfair to give my readers an

[1] For a very sensible explanation of nudity and
bathing see Finck's *Lotos Time* in *Japan*, pp. 286–
297.

idea that masculinity alone was our highest
ideal for woman. Far from it! Accomplishments and the gentler graces of life were
required of them. Music, dancing, and literature were not neglected. Some of the finest
verses in our literature were expressions of
feminine sentiments; in fact, woman played
an important rôle in the history of Japanese
belles-lettres. Dancing was taught (I am
speaking of samurai girls and not of *geisha*)
only to smooth the angularity of their move-
ments. Music was to regale the weary hours
of their fathers and husbands; hence it was
not for the technique, the art as such, that
music was learned; for the ultimate object
was purification of heart, since it was said
that no harmony of sound is attainable without the player's heart being in harmony with
itself. Here again we see the same idea prevailing which we notice in the training of
youths—that accomplishments were ever kept
subservient to moral worth. Just enough
of music and dancing to add grace and
brightness to life, but never to foster vanity

and extravagance. I sympathise with the Persian Prince, who, when taken into a ball-room in London and asked to take part in the merriment, bluntly remarked that in his country they provided a particular set of girls to do that kind of business for them.

The accomplishments of our women were not acquired for show or social ascendancy. They were a home diversion; and if they shone in social parties, it was as the attributes of a hostess,—in other words, as a part of the household contrivance for hospitality. Domesticity guided their education. It may be said that the accomplishments of the women of Old Japan, be they martial or pacific in character, were mainly intended for the home; and, however far they might roam, they never lost sight of the hearth as the centre. It was to maintain its honour and integrity that they slaved, drudged, and gave up their lives. Night and day, in tones at once firm and tender, brave and plaintive, they sang to their little nests. As daughter, woman sacrificed herself for her father, as wife

for her husband, and as mother for her son.
Thus from earliest youth she was taught to
deny herself. Her life was not one of independence, but of dependent service. Man's
helpmeet, if her presence is helpful she stays
on the stage with him: if it hinders his work,
she retires behind the curtain. Not infrequently does it happen that a youth becomes
enamoured of a maiden who returns his love
with equal ardour, but, when she realises his
interest in her makes him forgetful of his
duties, disfigures her person that her attrac-
tions may cease. Adzuma, the ideal wife in
the minds of samurai girls, finds herself loved
by a man who is conspiring against her husband. Upon pretence of joining in the
guilty plot, she manages in the dark to take
her husband's place, and the sword of the
lover-assassin descends upon her own devoted head. The following epistle written by
the wife of a young daimio, before taking her
own life, needs no comment:

"I have heard that no accident or chance ever
mars the march of events here below, and that all

is in accordance with a plan. To take shelter under a common bough or a drink of the same river, is alike ordained from ages prior to our birth. Since we were joined in ties of eternal wedlock, now two short years ago, my heart hath followed thee, even as its shadow followeth an object, inseparably bound heart to heart, loving and being loved. Learning but recently, however, that the coming battle is to be the last of thy labour and life, take the farewell greeting of thy loving partner. I have heard that Kowu, the mighty warrior of ancient China, lost a battle, loth to part with his favorite Gu. Yoshinaka, too, brave as he was, brought disaster to his cause, too weak to bid prompt farewell to his wife. Why should I, to whom earth no longer offers hope or joy—Why should I detain thee or thy thoughts by living? Why should I not, rather, await thee on the road which all mortal kind must sometime tread? Never, prithee, never, forget the many benefits which our good master Hidéyori hath heaped upon thee. The gratitude we owe him is as deep as the sea and as high as the hills."

Woman's surrender of herself to the good of her husband, home, and family, was as willing and honourable as the man's self-surrender to the good of his lord and country. Self-renunciation, without which no life-enigma can be solved, was the key-note of the loyalty of man as well as of the domes-

ticity of woman. She was no more the slave
of man than was her husband of his liege-
lord, and the part she played was recognised
as *naijo*, "the inner help." In the ascending
scale of service stood woman, who annihilated
herself for man, that he might annihilate himself for the master, that he in turn might obey
Heaven. I know the weakness of this teaching and that the superiority of Christianity
is nowhere more manifested than here, in
that it requires of each and every living soul
direct responsibility to its Creator. Nevertheless, as far as the doctrine of service—the
serving of a cause higher than one's own self,
even at the sacrifice of one's individuality;
I say the doctrine of service, which is the
greatest that Christ preached and was the
sacred key-note of His mission—so far as that
is concerned, Bushido was based on eternal
truth.

My readers will not accuse me of undue
prejudice in favour of slavish surrender of
volition. I accept in a large measure the
view advanced and defended with breadth of

learning and profundity of thought by Hegel, that history is the unfolding and realisation of freedom. The point I wish to make is that the whole teaching of Bushido was so thoroughly imbued with the spirit of self-sacrifice, that it was required not only of woman but of man. Hence, until the influence of its precepts is entirely done away with, our society will not realise the view rashly expressed by an American exponent of woman's rights, who exclaimed, "May all the daughters of Japan rise in revolt against ancient customs!" Can such a revolt succeed? Will it improve the female status? Will the rights they gain by such a summary process repay the loss of that sweetness of disposition, that gentleness of manner, which are their present heritage? Was not the loss of domesticity on the part of Roman matrons followed by moral corruption too gross to mention? Can the American reformer assure us that a revolt of our daughters is the true course for their historical development to take? These are grave questions. Changes

must and will come without revolts!   In the
meantime let us see whether the status of the
fair sex under the Bushido regimen was really
so bad as to justify a revolt.

We hear much of the outward respect European knights paid to "God and the ladies,"
—the incongruity of the two terms making
Gibbon blush; we are also told by Hallam
that the morality of chivalry was coarse, that
gallantry implied illicit love.   The effect of
chivalry on the weaker vessel was food for
reflection on the part of philosophers, M.
Guizot contending that feudalism and chivalry wrought wholesome influences, while Mr.
Spencer tells us that in a militant society (and
what is feudal society if not militant?) the
position of woman is necessarily low, improv-
ing only as society becomes more industrial.
Now is M. Guizot's theory true of Japan, or
is Mr. Spencer's?   In reply I might aver that
both are right.   The military class in Japan
was restricted to the samurai, comprising
nearly two million souls.   Above them were
the military nobles, the *daimio*, and the

court nobles, the *kugé*—these higher, sybariti-
cal nobles being fighters only in name.   Below them were masses of the common people—mechanics, tradesmen, and peasants—
whose life was devoted to arts of peace.   Thus
what Herbert Spencer gives as the characteristics of a militant type of society may be
said to have been exclusively confined to the
samurai class, while those of the industrial
type were applicable to the classes above and
below it.   This is well illustrated by the
position of woman; for in no class did she
experience less freedom than among the samurai.   Strange to say, the lower the social
class—as, for instance, among small artisans
—the more equal was the position of husband
and wife.   Among the higher nobility, too,
the difference in the relations of the sexes
was less marked, chiefly because there were
few occasions to bring the differences of sex
into prominence, the leisurely nobleman having become literally effeminate.   Thus Spencer's dictum was fully exemplified in Old
Japan.   As to Guizot's, those who read his

presentation of a feudal community will remember that he had the higher nobility
especially under consideration, so that his
generalisation applies to the *daimio* and the
kugé.

I shall be guilty of gross injustice to historical truth if my words give one a very low
opinion of the status of woman under Bushido.
I do not hesitate to state that she was not
treated as man's equal; but, until we learn
to discriminate between differences and in-
equalities, there will always be misunder-
standings upon this subject.

When we think in how few respects men
are equal among themselves, *e. g.*, before law
courts or voting polls, it seems idle to trouble
ourselves with a discussion on the equality
of sexes. When the American Declaration of
Independence said that all men were created
equal, it had no reference to their mental or
physical gifts; it simply repeated what Ulpian
long ago announced, that before the law all
men are equal. Legal rights were in this
case the measure of their equality. Were the

law the only scale by which to measure the
position of woman in a community, it would
be as easy to tell where she stands as to give
her avoirdupois in pounds and ounces. But
the question is: Is there a correct standard
in comparing the relative social position of
the sexes? Is it right, is it enough, to compare woman's status to man's, as the value
of silver is compared with that of gold, and
give the ratio numerically? Such a method
of calculation excludes from consideration the
most important kind of value which a human
being possesses, namely, the intrinsic. In
view of the manifold variety of requisites for
making each sex fulfil its earthly mission, the
standard to be adopted in measuring its relative position must be of a composite character; or to borrow from economic language, it
must be a multiple standard. Bushido had a
standard of its own and it was binomial. It
tried to gauge the value of woman on the
battle-field and by the hearth. There she
counted for very little; here for all. The
treatment accorded her corresponded to this

double measurement:—as a social-political unit not much, while as wife and mother she received highest respect and deepest affection. Why, among so military a nation as the Romans, were their matrons so highly venerated? Was it not because they were *matrona*, mothers? Not as fighters or lawgivers, but as their mothers did men bow before them. So with us. While fathers and husbands were absent in field or camp, the government of the household was left entirely in the hands of mothers and wives. The education of the young, even their defence, was entrusted to them. The warlike exercises of women, of which I have spoken, were primarily to enable them intelligently to direct and follow the education of their children.

I have noticed a rather superficial notion prevailing among half-informed foreigners, that because the common Japanese expression for one's wife is "my rustic wife" and the like, she is despised and held in little esteem. When it is told that such phrases as "my

foolish father," "my swinish son," "my awk-
ward self," etc., are in current use, is not the
answer clear enough?

To me it seems that our idea of marital
union goes in some ways farther than the so-
called Christian. "Man and woman shall be
one flesh." The individualism of the Anglo-
Saxon cannot let go of the idea that husband
and wife are two persons;—hence when they
disagree, their separate *rights* are recognised,
and when they agree, they exhaust their
vocabulary in all sorts of silly pet-names and
nonsensical blandishments. It sounds highly
irrational to our ears, when a husband or
wife speaks to a third party of his or her
other half—better or worse—as being lovely,
bright, kind, and what not. Is it good taste
to speak of one's self as "my bright self,"
"my lovely disposition," and so forth? We
think praising one's own wife is praising a
part of one's own self, and self-praise is regarded, to say the least, as bad taste among
us,—and I hope, among Christian nations
too! I have diverged at some length be-

cause the polite debasement of one's consort was a usage most in vogue among the samurai.

The Teutonic races beginning their tribal life with a superstitious awe of the fair sex (though this is really wearing off in Germany!), and the Americans beginning their social life under the painful consciousness of the numerical insufficiency of women [1] (who, now increasing, are, I am afraid, fast losing the prestige their colonial mothers enjoyed), the respect man pays to woman has in Western civilisation become the chief standard of morality. But in the martial ethics of Bushido, the main water-shed dividing the good and the bad was sought elsewhere. It was located along the line of duty which bound man to his own divine soul and then to other souls in the five relations I have mentioned in the early part of this paper. Of these, we have brought to our reader's notice loyalty,

---

[1] I refer to those days when girls were imported from England and given in marriage for so many pounds of tobacco, etc.

the relation between one man as vassal and another as lord. Upon the rest, I have only dwelt incidentally as occasion presented itself; because they were not peculiar to Bushido. Being founded on natural affections, they could but be common to all mankind, though in some particulars they may have been accentuated by conditions which its teachings induced. In this connection there comes before me the peculiar strength and tenderness of friendship between man and man, which often added to the bond of brotherhood a romantic attachment doubtless intensified by the separation of the sexes in youth, — a separation which denied to affection the natural channel open to it in Western chivalry or in the free intercourse of Anglo-Saxon lands. I might fill pages with Japanese versions of the story of Damon and Pythias or Achilles and Patroclos, or tell in Bushido parlance of ties as sympathetic as those which bound David and Jonathan.

It is not surprising, however, that the virtues and teachings unique in the Precepts of Knighthood did not remain circumscribed to the military class. This makes us hasten to the consideration of the influence of Bushido on the nation at large.

CHAPTER XV

THUS far we have brought into view only a few of the more prominent peaks which rise above the range of knightly virtues, in themselves so much more elevated then the general level of our national life. As the sun in its rising first tips the highest peaks with russet hue, and then gradually casts its rays on the valley below, so the ethical system which first enlightened the military order drew in course of time followers from amongst the masses. Democracy raises up a natural prince for its leader, and aristocracy infuses a princely spirit among the people. Virtues are no less contagious than vices. "There needs but one wise man in a company, and all are wise, so rapid is the contagion," says Emerson. No social class or caste can resist the diffusive power of moral influence.

Prate as we may of the triumphant march of Anglo-Saxon liberty, rarely has it received impetus from the masses. Was it not rather the work of the squires and *gentlemen* ? Very truly does M. Taine say, "These three syllables, as used across the channel, summarise the history of English society." Democracy may make self-confident retorts to such a statement and fling back the question— "When Adam delved and Eve span, where then was the gentleman?" All the more pity that a gentleman was not present in Eden! The first parents missed him sorely and paid a high price for his absence. Had he been there, not only would the garden have been more tastefully dressed, but they would have learned without painful experience that disobedience to Jehovah was disloyalty and dishonour, treason and rebellion.

What Japan was she owed to the samurai. They were not only the flower of the nation, but its root as well. All the gracious gifts of

Heaven flowed through them. Though they kept themselves socially aloof from the populace, they set a moral standard for them and guided them by their example. I admit Bushido had its esoteric and exoteric teachings; these were eudemonic, looking after the welfare and happiness of the commonalty; those were aretaic, emphasising the practice of virtues for their own sake.

In the most chivalrous days of Europe, knights formed numerically but a small fraction of the population, but, as Emerson says, —"In English literature half the drama and all the novels, from Sir Philip Sidney to Sir Walter Scott, paint this figure (gentleman)." Write in place of Sidney and Scott, Chikamatsu and Bakin, and you have in a nutshell the main features of the literary history of Japan.

The innumerable avenues of popular amusement and instruction—the theatres, the story-tellers' booths, the preacher's dais, the musical recitations, the novels,—have taken for their chief theme the stories of the samurai.

The peasants around the open fire in their huts never tire of repeating the achievements of Yoshitsuné and his faithful retainer Benkéi, or of the two brave Soga brothers; the dusky urchins listen with gaping mouths until the last stick burns out and the fire dies in its embers, still leaving their hearts aglow with tale that is told. The clerks and the shop boys, after their day's work is over and the *amado* [1] of the store are closed, gather together to relate the story of Nobunaga and Hidéyoshi far into the night, until slumber overtakes their weary eyes and transports them from the drudgery of the counter to the exploits of the field. The very babe just beginning to toddle is taught to lisp the adventures of Momotaro, the daring conqueror of ogreland. Even girls are so imbued with the love of knightly deeds and virtues that, like Desdemona, they would seriously incline to devour with greedy ear the romance of the samurai.

The samurai grew to be the *beau ideal* of

[1] Outside shutters.

the whole race. "As among flowers the
cherry is queen, so among men the samurai
is lord," so sang the populace. Debarred
from commercial pursuits, the military class
itself did not aid commerce; but there was
no channel of human activity, no avenue of
thought, which did not receive in some measure an impetus from Bushido. Intellectual
and moral Japan was directly or indirectly
the work of Knighthood.

Mr. Mallock, in his exceedingly suggestive
book, *Aristocracy and Evolution*, has elo-
quently told us that "social evolution, in so
far as it is other than biological, may be defined as the unintended result of the inten-
tions of great men"; further, that historical
progress is produced by a struggle "not
among the community generally, to live, but
a struggle amongst a small section of the
community to lead, to direct, to employ,
the majority in the best way." Whatever may be said about the soundness of
his argument, these statements are amply
verified in the part played by bushi in the

social progress, so far as it went, of our Empire.

How the spirit of Bushido permeated all social classes is also shown in the development of a certain order of men, known as *otoko-daté*, the natural leaders of democracy. Staunch fellows were they, every inch of them strong with the strength of massive manhood. At once the spokesmen and the guardians of popular rights, they had each a following of hundreds and thousands of souls who proffered, in the same fashion that samurai did to *daimio*, the willing service of "limb and life, of body, chattels, and earthly honour." Backed by a vast multitude of rash and impetuous working men, these born " bosses " formed a formidable check to the rampancy of the two-sworded order.

In manifold ways has Bushido filtered down from the social class where it originated, and acted as leaven among the masses, furnishing a moral standard for the whole people. The Precepts of Knighthood, begun at first as the glory of the *élite*, became in time an aspiration and inspiration to the nation at large; and though the populace could not attain the moral height of those loftier souls, yet *Yamato Damashii*, the Soul of Japan, ultimately came to express the *Volksgeist* of the Island Realm. If religion is no more than "Morality touched by emotion," as Matthew Arnold defines it, few ethical systems are better entitled to the rank of religion than Bushido. Motoöri has put the mute utterance of the nation into words when he sings:

> "Isles of blest Japan!
>   Should your Yamato spirit
>   Strangers seek to scan,
>   Say—scenting morn's sunlit air,
>   Blows the cherry wild and fair!"

Yes, the *sakura* [1] has for ages been the favourite of our people and the emblem of our character. Mark particularly the terms of definition which the poet uses, the words the *wild cherry flower scenting the morning sun*.

The Yamato spirit is not a tame, tender

---

[1] *Cerasus pseudo-cerasus*, Lindley.

plant, but a wild—in the sense of natural—growth; it is indigenous to the soil; its accidental qualities it may share with the flowers of other lands, but in its essence it remains the original, spontaneous outgrowth of our clime. But its nativity is not its sole claim to our affection. The refinement and grace of its beauty appeal to *our* æsthetic sense as no other flower can. We cannot share the admiration of the Europeans for their roses, which lack the simplicity of our flower. Then, too, the thorns that are hidden beneath the sweetness of the rose, the tenacity with which she clings to life, as though loth or afraid to die rather than drop untimely, preferring to rot on her stem; her showy colours and heavy odours—all these are traits so unlike our flower, which carries no dagger or poison under its beauty, which is ever ready to depart life at the call of nature, whose colours are never gorgeous, and whose light fragrance never palls. Beauty of colour and of form is limited in its showing; it is a fixed quality of existence, whereas fragrance is volatile, ethereal as the breathing of life. So in all religious ceremonies frankincense and myrrh play a prominent part. There is something spirituelle in redolence. When the delicious perfume of the sakura quickens the morning air, as the sun in its course rises to illumine first the isles of the Far East, few sensations are more serenely exhilarating than to inhale, as it were, the very breath of beauteous day.

When the Creator Himself is pictured as making new resolutions in His heart upon smelling a sweet savour (Gen. viii. 21), is it any wonder that the sweet-smelling season of the cherry blossom should call forth the whole nation from their little habitations? Blame them not, if for a time their limbs forget their toil and moil and their hearts their pangs and sorrows. Their brief pleasure ended, they return to their daily task with new strength and new resolutions. Thus in ways more than one is the sakura the flower of the nation.

Is, then, this flower, so sweet and evanescent, blown whithersoever the wind listeth, and, shedding a puff of perfume, ready to vanish forever, is this flower the type of the Yamato spirit? Is the soul of Japan so frailly mortal?

CHAPTER XVI

IS BUSHIDO STILL ALIVE?

HAS Western civilisation, in its march through our land, already wiped out every trace of its ancient discipline? It were a sad thing if a nation's soul could die so fast. That were a poor soul that could succumb so easily to extraneous influences.

The aggregate of psychological elements which constitute a national character is as tenacious as the "irreducible elements of species, of the fins of the fish, of the beak of the bird, of the tooth of the carnivorous animal." In his recent book, full of shallow asseverations and brilliant generalisations, M. LeBon [1] says: "The discoveries due to the intelligence are the common patrimony of humanity; qualities or defects of character

[1] *The Psychology of Peoples*, p. 33.

constitute the exclusive patrimony of each people: they are the firm rock which the waters must wash day by day for centuries, before they can wear away even its external asperities." These are strong words and would be highly worth pondering over, provided there were qualities and defects of character which *constitute the exclusive patrimony* of each people. Schematising theories of this sort had been advanced long before Le-Bon began to write his book, and they were exploded long ago by Theodor Waitz and Hugh Murray. In studying the various virtues instilled by Bushido, we have drawn upon European sources for comparison and illustrations, and we have seen that no one quality of character was its *exclusive* patrimony. It is true the aggregate of moral qualities presents a quite unique aspect. It is this aggregate which Emerson names a "compound result into which every great force enters as an ingredient." But, instead of making it, as LeBon does, an exclusive patrimony of a race or people, the Concord philosopher calls it "an element which unites the most forcible persons of every country; makes them intelligible and agreeable to each other; and is somewhat so precise that it is at once felt if an individual lack the Masonic sign."

The character which Bushido stamped on our nation and on the samurai in particular, cannot be said to form "an irreducible element of species," but nevertheless as to the vitality which it retains there is no doubt. Were Bushido a mere physical force, the momentum it has gained in the last seven hundred years could not stop so abruptly. Were it transmitted only by heredity, its influence must be immensely widespread. Just think, as M. Cheysson, a French economist, has calculated, that, supposing there be three generations in a century, "each of us would have in his veins the blood of at least twenty millions of the people living in the year 1000 A.D." The merest peasant that grubs the soil, "bowed by the weight of centuries," has in his veins the blood of ages, and is thus brother to us as much as "to the ox."

An unconscious and irresistible power, Bushido has been moving the nation and individuals. It was an honest confession of the race when Yoshida Shôin, one of the most brilliant pioneers of Modern Japan, wrote on the eve of his execution the following stanza:

"Full well I knew this course must end in death;
  It was Yamato spirit urged me on
  To dare whate'er betide."

Unformulated, Bushido was and still is the animating spirit, the motor force of our country.

Mr. Ransome says that "there are three distinct Japans in existence side by side to-day,—the old, which has not wholly died out; the new, hardly yet born except in spirit; and the transition, passing now through its most critical throes." While this is very true in most respects, and particularly as regards tangible and concrete institutions, the statement, as applied to fundamental ethical notions, requires some modification; for

Bushido, the maker and product of Old Japan, is still the guiding principle of the transition and will prove the formative force of the new era.

The great statesmen who steered the ship of our state through the hurricane of the Restoration and the whirlpool of national rejuvenation, were men who knew no other moral teaching than the Precepts of Knighthood. Some writers [1] have lately tried to prove that the Christian missionaries contributed an appreciable quota to the making of New Japan. I would fain render honour to whom honour is due; but this honour can as yet hardly be accorded to the good missionaries. More fitting it will be to their profession to stick to the scriptural injunction of preferring one another in honour, than to advance a claim in which they have no proofs to back them. For myself, I believe that Christian missionaries are doing great things

---

[1] Speer: *Missions and Politics in Asia*, Lecture IV., pp. 189–192; Dennis: *Christian Missions and Social Progress*, vol. i., p. 32, vol. ii., 70, etc.

for Japan—in the domain of education, and especially of moral education:—only, the mysterious though not the less certain working of the Spirit is still hidden in divine secrecy. Whatever they do is still of indirect effect. No, as yet Christian missions have effected but little visible in moulding the character of New Japan. No, it was Bushido, pure and simple, that urged us on for weal or woe. Open the biographies of the makers of Modern Japan—of Sakuma, of Saigo, of Okubo, of Kido, not to mention the reminiscences of living men such as Ito, Okuma, Itagaki, etc.,—and you will find that it was under the impetus of samuraihood that they thought and wrought. When Mr. Henry Norman declared, after his study and observation of the Far East, that the only respect in which Japan differed from other oriental despotisms lay in "the ruling influence among her people of the strictest, loftiest, and the most punctilious codes of honour that man has ever devised," he touched the mainspring which has made New Japan what she is, and which will make her what she is destined to be.[1]

The transformation of Japan is a fact patent to the whole world. Into a work of such magnitude various motives naturally entered; but if one were to name the principal, one would not hesitate to name Bushido. When we opened the whole country to foreign trade, when we introduced the latest improvements in every department of life, when we began to study Western politics and sciences, our guiding motive was not the development of our physical resources and the increase of wealth; much less was it a blind imitation of Western customs.

A close observer of oriental institutions and peoples has written:

"We are told every day how Europe has influenced Japan, and forget that the change in those islands was entirely self-generated, that Europeans did not teach Japan, but that Japan of herself chose to learn from Europe methods of organisation, civil and military, which have so far proved successful. She imported European mechanical science, as the

[1] *The Far East*, p. 375.

Turks years before imported European artillery. That is not exactly influence," continues Mr. Townsend, "unless, indeed, England is influenced by purchasing tea in China. Where is the European apostle," asks our author, "or philosopher or statesman or agitator, who has re-made Japan?"[1]

Mr. Townsend has well perceived that the spring of action which brought about the changes in Japan lay entirely within our own selves; and if he had only probed into our psychology, his keen powers of observation would easily have convinced him that this spring was no other than Bushido. The sense of honour which cannot bear being looked down upon as an inferior power,— that was the strongest of motives. Pecuniary or industrial considerations were awakened later in the process of transformation.

The influence of Bushido is still so palpable that he who runs may read. A glimpse into Japanese life will make it manifest. Read Hearn, the most eloquent and truthful interpreter of the Japanese mind, and you see the working of that mind to be an example of the

[1] Meredith Townsend, *Asia and Europe*, p. 28.

working of Bushido. The universal politeness of the people, which is the legacy of
knightly ways, is too well known to be repeated anew. The physical endurance, fortitude, and bravery that "the little Jap"
possesses, were sufficiently proved in the
Chino-Japanese war.[1] "Is there any nation
more loyal and patriotic?" is a question asked
by many; and for the proud answer, "There
is not," we must thank the Precepts of
Knighthood.

On the other hand, it is fair to recognise
that for the very faults and defects of our
character, Bushido is largely responsible.
Our lack of abstruse philosophy—while some
of our young men have already gained international reputation in scientific researches,
not one has achieved anything in philosophical lines—is traceable to the neglect of meta-
physical training under Bushido's regimen of
education. Our sense of honour is responsible

[1] Among other works on the subject, read East-
lake and Yamada on *Heroic Japan*, and Diosy on
The New Far East.

for our exaggerated sensitiveness and touchiness; and if there is the conceit in us with which some foreigners charge us, that, too, is a pathological outcome of honour.

Have you seen in your tour of Japan many a young man with unkempt hair, dressed in shabbiest garb, carrying in his hand a large cane or a book, stalking about the streets with an air of utter indifference to mundane things? He is the *shoséi* (student), to whom the earth is too small and the heavens are not high enough. He has his own theories of the universe and of life. He dwells in castles of air and feeds on ethereal words of wisdom. In his eyes beams the fire of ambition; his mind is athirst for knowledge. Penury is only a stimulus to drive him onward; worldly goods are in his sight shackles to his character. He is the repository of loyalty and patriotism. He is the self-imposed guardian of national honour. With all his virtues and his faults, he is the last fragment of Bushido.

Deep-rooted and powerful as is still the

effect of Bushido, I have said that it is an
unconscious and mute influence. The heart
of the people responds, without knowing a
reason why, to any appeal made to what it
has inherited, and hence the same moral idea
expressed in a newly translated term and in
an old Bushido term, has a vastly different
degree of efficacy. A backsliding Christian,
whom no pastoral persuasion could help from
downward tendency, was reverted from his
course by an appeal made to his loyalty, the
fidelity he once swore to his Master. The
word "Loyalty" revived all the noble sentiments that were permitted to grow lukewarm.
A party of unruly youths engaged in a long-
continued "students' strike" in a college, on
account of their dissatisfaction with a certain
teacher, disbanded at two simple questions
put by the Director,—"Is your professor a
worthy character? If so, you ought to respect him and keep him in the school. Is he
weak? If so, it is not manly to push a falling man." The scientific incapacity of the
professor, which was the beginning of the

trouble, dwindled into insignificance in comparison with the moral issues hinted at. By arousing the sentiments nurtured by Bushido, moral renovation of great magnitude can be accomplished.

One cause of the failure of mission work is that most of the missionaries are entirely ignorant of our history—"What do we care for heathen records?" some say—and consequently estrange their religion from the habits of thought we and our forefathers have been accustomed to for centuries past. Mocking a nation's history?—as though the career of any people—even of the lowest African savages possessing no record—were not a page in the general history of mankind, written by the hand of God Himself. The very lost races are a palimpsest to be deciphered by a seeing eye. To a philosophic and pious mind the races themselves are marks of Divine chirography clearly traced in black and white as on their skin; and if this simile holds good, the yellow race forms a precious page inscribed in hieroglyphics of gold!

Ignoring the past career of a people, missionaries claim that Christianity is a new religion, whereas, to my mind, it is an "old, old story," which, if presented in intelligible words,—that is to say, if expressed in the vocabulary familiar in the moral development of a people, —will find easy lodgment in their hearts, irrespective of race or nationality. Christianity in its American or English form—with more of Anglo-Saxon freaks and fancies than grace and purity of its Founder—is a poor scion to graft on Bushido stock. Should the propagator of the new faith uproot the entire stock, root, and branches, and plant the seeds of the Gospel on the ravaged soil? Such a heroic process may be possible—in Hawaii, where, it is alleged, the Church militant had complete success in amassing spoils of wealth itself, and in annihilating the aboriginal race; such a process is most decidedly impossible in Japan—nay, it is a process which Jesus Himself would never have adopted in founding His kingdom on earth.

It behooves us to take more to heart the

following words of a saintly man, devout Christian, and profound scholar:

"Men have divided the world into heathen and Christian, without considering how much good may have been hidden in the one or how much evil may have been mingled with the other. They have compared the best part of themselves with the worst of their neighbours, the ideal of Christianity with the corruption of Greece or of the East. They have not aimed at impartiality, but have been contented to accumulate all that could be said in praise of their own, and in dispraise of other forms of religion." [1]

But, whatever may be the error committed by individuals, there is little doubt that the fundamental principle of the religion they profess is a power which we must take into account in reckoning the future of Bushido, whose days seem to be already numbered. Ominous signs are in the air that betoken its future. Not only signs, but redoubtable forces are at work to threaten it.

[1] Jowett, *Sermons on Faith and Doctrine*, ii.

CHAPTER XVII

FEW historical comparisons can be more judiciously made than between the Chivalry of Europe and the Bushido of Japan, and, if history repeats itself, it certainly will do with the fate of the latter what it did with that of the former. The particular and local causes for the decay of chivalry which St. Palaye gives, have, of course, little application to Japanese conditions; but the larger and more general causes that helped to undermine knighthood and chivalry in and after the Middle Ages are as surely working for the decline of Bushido.

One remarkable difference between the experience of Europe and of Japan is, that whereas in Europe, when chivalry was weaned from feudalism and was adopted by the

Church, it obtained a fresh lease of life, in
Japan no religion was large enough to nourish it; hence, when the mother institution,
feudalism, was gone, Bushido, left an orphan,
had to shift for itself.   The present elaborate
military organisation might take it under its
patronage, but we know that modern warfare
can afford little room for its continuous
growth.   Shintoism, which fostered it in its
infancy, is itself superannuated.   The hoary
sages of ancient China are being supplanted
by the intellectual parvenu of the type of
Bentham and Mill.   Moral theories of a
comfortable kind, flattering to the Chauvin-
istic tendencies of the time, and therefore
thought well adapted to the need of this
day, have been invented and propounded;
but as yet we hear only their shrill voices
echoing through the columns of yellow
journalism.

Principalities and powers are arrayed
against the Precepts of Knighthood.   Already, as Veblen says, "the decay of the
ceremonial code—or, as it is otherwise called,

the vulgarisation of life—among the industrial classes proper, has become one of the chief enormities of latter-day civilisation in the eyes of all persons of delicate sensibilities." The irresistible tide of triumphant democracy, which can tolerate no form or shape of trust,—and Bushido was a trust organised by those who monopolised reserve capital of intellect and culture, fixing the grades and value of moral qualities,—is alone powerful enough to engulf the remnant of Bushido. The present societary forces are antagonistic to petty class spirit, and chivalry is, as Freeman severely criticises, a class spirit. Modern society, if it pretends to any unity, cannot admit "purely personal obligations devised in the interests of an exclusive class." [1] Add to this the progress of popular instruction, of industrial arts and habits, of wealth and city-life,—then we can easily see that neither the keenest cuts of samurai sword nor the sharpest shafts shot from Bushido's boldest bows can aught avail. The state built upon the

[1] *Norman Conquest*, vol. v., p. 482.

rock of Honour and fortified by the same—
shall we call it the *Ehrenstaat*, or, after the
manner of Carlyle, the Heroarchy?—is fast
falling into the hands of quibbling lawyers
and gibbering politicians armed with logic-
chopping engines of war. The words which a
great thinker used in speaking of Theresa
and Antigone may aptly be repeated of
the samurai, that "the medium in which
their ardent deeds took shape is forever
gone."

Alas for knightly virtues! alas for samurai
pride! Morality ushered into the world with
the sound of bugles and drums, is destined
to fade away as "the captains and the kings
depart."

If history can teach us anything, the state
built on martial virtues—be it a city like
Sparta or an Empire like Rome—can never
make on earth a "continuing city." Universal and natural as is the fighting instinct in
man, fruitful as it has proved to be of noble
sentiments and manly virtues, it does not
comprehend the whole man. Beneath the

instinct to fight there lurks a diviner instinct
—to love. We have seen that Shintoism, Mencius, and Wan Yang Ming, have all clearly
taught it; but Bushido and all other militant
types of ethics, engrossed doubtless, with
questions of immediate practical need, too
often forgot duly to emphasise this fact.
Life has grown larger in these latter times.
Callings nobler and broader than a warrior's
claim our attention to-day. With an en-
larged view of life, with the growth of democracy, with better knowledge of other
peoples and nations, the Confucian idea of
benevolence—dare I also add the Buddhist
idea of pity?—will expand into the Christian
conception of love. Men have become more
than subjects, having grown to the estate
of citizens; nay, they are more than citizens
—being men. Though war clouds hang
heavy upon our horizon, we will believe
that the wings of the angel of peace can
disperse them. The history of the world
confirms the prophecy that " the meek
shall inherit the earth." A nation that sells

its birthright of peace, and backslides from
the front rank of industrialism into the
file of fillibusterism, makes a poor bargain
indeed!

When the conditions of society are so
changed that they have become not only
adverse but hostile to Bushido, it is time for
it to prepare for an honourable burial. It is
just as difficult to point out when chivalry
dies, as to determine the exact time of its
inception. Dr. Miller says that chivalry was
formally abolished in the year 1559, when
Henry II. of France was slain in a tourna-
ment. With us, the edict formally abolish-
ing feudalism in 1870 was the signal to toll
the knell of Bushido. The edict, issued five
years later, prohibiting the wearing of swords,
rang out the old, "the unbought grace of life,
the cheap defence of nations, the nurse of
manly sentiment and heroic enterprise," it
rang in the new age of "sophisters, economists, and calculators."

It has been said that Japan won her late
war with China by means of Murata guns and

Krupp cannon; it has been said the victory
was the work of a modern school-system;
but these are less than half-truths. Does
ever a piano, be it of the choicest workman-
ship of Ehrbar or Steinway burst forth into
the Rhapsodies of Liszt or the Sonatas of
Beethoven, without a master's hand? Or, if
guns win battles, why did not Louis Napoleon
beat the Prussians with his *Mitrailleuse*, or
the Spaniards with their Mausers the Fili-
pinos, whose arms were no better than the old-
fashioned Remingtons? Needless to repeat
what has grown a trite saying,—that it is
the spirit that quickeneth, without which the
best of implements profiteth but little. The
most improved guns and cannon do not shoot
of their own accord; the most modern educa-
tional system does not make a coward a hero.
No! What won the battles on the Yalu, in
Corea and Manchuria, were the ghosts of our
fathers, guiding our hands and beating in our
hearts. They are not dead, those ghosts, the
spirits of our warlike ancestors. To those who
have eyes to see, they are clearly visible.

Scratch a Japanese of the most advanced
ideas, and he will show a samurai. The great
inheritance of honour, of valour, and of all
martial virtues is, as Professor Cramb very
fitly expresses it, "but ours on trust, the fief
inalienable of the dead and of the generations
to come," and the summons of the present
is to guard this heritage, nor to bate one
jot of the ancient spirit ; the summons of
the future will be so to widen its scope as
to apply it in all walks and relations of
life.

It has been predicted—and predictions
have been corroborated by the events of the
last half-century—that the moral system of
Feudal Japan, like its castles and its ar-
mouries, will crumble into dust, and new
ethics rise phœnix-like to lead New Japan in
her path of progress. Desirable and probable
as the fulfilment of such a prophecy is, we
must not forget that a phœnix rises only from
its own ashes, and that it is not a bird of
passage, neither does it fly on pinions borrowed from other birds. "The Kingdom of

God is within you." It does not come roll-
ing down the mountains, however lofty; it
does not come sailing across the seas, however
broad. "God has granted," says the Koran,
"to every people a prophet in its own tongue."
The seeds of the Kingdom, as vouched for
and apprehended by the Japanese mind,
blossomed in Bushido. Now its days are
closing—sad to say, before its full fruition—
and we turn in every direction for other
sources of sweetness and light, of strength and
comfort, but among them there is as yet
nothing found to take its place. The profit-
and-loss philosophy of utilitarians and mat-
erialists finds favour among logic-choppers
with half a soul. The only other ethical system which is powerful enough to cope with
utilitarianism and materialism is Christianity, in comparison with which Bushido, it
must be confessed, is like "a dimly burning
wick" which the Messiah was proclaimed not
to quench, but to fan into a flame. Like
His Hebrew precursors, the prophets—notably Isaiah, Jeremiah, Amos, and Habakkuk

—Bushido laid particular stress on the moral conduct of rulers and public men and of nations, whereas the ethics of Christ, which deal almost solely with individuals and His personal followers, will find more and more practical application as individualism, in its capacity of a moral factor, grows in potency. The domineering, self - assertive, so - called master-morality of Nietsche, itself akin in some respects to Bushido, is, if I am not greatly mistaken, a passing phase or temporary reaction against what he terms, by morbid distortion, the humble, self-denying slave-morality of the Nazarene.

Christianity and materialism (including utilitarianism)—or will the future reduce them to still more archaic forms of Hebraism and Hellenism?—will divide the world between them. Lesser systems of morals will ally themselves to either side for their preservation. On which side will Bushido enlist? Having no set dogma or formula to defend, it can afford to disappear as an entity; like the cherry blossom, it is willing to die at the first gust of the morning breeze. But a total extinction will never be its lot. Who can say that stoicism is dead? It is dead as a system; but it is alive as a virtue: its energy and vitality are still felt through many channels of life—in the philosophy of Western nations, in the jurisprudence of all the civilised world. Nay, wherever man struggles to raise himself above himself, wherever his spirit masters his flesh by his own exertions, there we see the immortal discipline of Zeno at work.

Bushido as an independent code of ethics may vanish, but its power will not perish from the earth; its schools of martial prowess or civic honour may be demolished, but its light and its glory will long survive their ruins. Like its symbolic flower, after it is blown to the four winds, it will still bless mankind with the perfume with which it will enrich life. Ages after, when its customaries will have been buried and its very name forgotten, its odours will come floating in the air as from a far-off, unseen hill, "the way-

side gaze beyond";—then in the beautiful
language of the Quaker poet,

> "The traveller owns the grateful sense
> Of sweetness near, he knows not whence,
> And, pausing, takes with forehead bare
> The benediction of the air."

INDEX

[In pronouncing Japanese names, use the Continental European sounds of vowels, and consonants according to the usual values in English, giving the hard sound of *g; e* at the end of a syllable, as in Nitobe, Shigemori, Tametomo, etc., is as *e* in *prey*. In some names, as in Iyéyasŭ (final *u* being short), we have used accents.]

A

B

E

F

G

H

TUTTLE PUBLISHING

A Member of the Periplus Publishing Group

Please return this card to receive a FREE catalog and to be placed on our mailing list.

Name _____

Address _____ Apt. # _____

City _____ State _____ Zip _____

Phone _____ Email _____

In which book was this card found? _____ Where purchased? _____

Have you ever visited our website? _____ Would you like to receive our electronic newsletter? _____

Comments (about the book, website, etc.): _____

Please check all subject areas of interest to you:

☐ Antiques and Collectibles   ☐ Art & Architecture   ☐ Asian Culture & History   ☐ Asian Literature & Poetry
  ☐ Cake Decorating   ☐ Children's   ☐ Cooking   ☐ Crafts & Games   ☐ Interior Design
  ☐ Feng Shui   ☐ Gardening & Nature   ☐ Health & Beauty   ☐ Language   ☐ Martial Arts
  ☐ Origami   ☐ Religion & Philosophy   ☐ Self-Help & Inspiration   ☐ Travel

Which magazines do you read on a regular basis? _____

Available wherever books are sold or call 1-800-526-2778, fax 1-800-329-8885

Email: info@tuttlepublishing.com

See our complete title listing and view our monthly promotions at www.tuttlepublishing.com

TUTTLE PUBLISHING

Airport Industrial Park

364 Innovation Drive

North Clarendon, VT 05759-9436

BIC100